Goodbye God

Goodbye God

12 STIRRING MESSAGES
by
W. P. NICHOLSON

Compiled by Stanley Barnes

AMBASSADOR

BELFAST ◆ **GREENVILLE**
NORTHERN IRELAND ▼ SOUTH CAROLINA

ISBN 1 84030 030 2

Ambassador Publications
a division of
Ambassador Productions Ltd.
Providence House
16 Hillview Avenue,
Belfast, BT5 6JR
Northern Ireland

Emerald House
1 Chick Springs Road, Suite 206
Greenville,
South Carolina 29609, USA

Contents

❖

Introduction 7

Goodbye God 9

The Necessity of Repentance 19

Regeneration 31

What must I do to be Saved? 49

Saved and Sure 57

Save Yourselves 67

Cross-Bearing 75

The Unpardonable Sin 85

The Great Judgment Day 103

Hell 119

Heaven 141

Christ's Second Coming 159

Introduction

---------- ❖ ----------

For over sixty years the Rev. W. P. Nicholson travelled the world preaching the Gospel. Like John Wesley, he cried 'the world is my parish.'

He was an evangelistic contemporary of R. A. Torrey, Billy Sunday, Dr. J. Wilbur Chapman and Mr. Charles M. Alexander. As a result of his United Gospel Campaigns in Ulster during the early 1920's, many thousands were brought to Christ.

Dr. Henry Montgomery of the Shankill Road Mission said of Nicholson's preaching:

'His sermons are often an hour long, and people listen with the most eager interest from beginning to end. They are thoroughly sound and scriptural. He preaches the new birth, conversion, the work of the Holy Spirit and separtion from the world with great force. The Spirit of God has evidently rested upon him in much power, for he delivers to the people, as he understands it, the whole counsel of God. He speaks of sin as the Bible views it; of salvation as the Bible gives it; and the power of the Gospel to deliver the slaves of evil from their cruel bondage for evermore.'

We are glad to commend these evangelistic sermons. They read easily, they challenge the heart and best of all they have been used to the salvation of souls. May the Holy Spirit cause them to burn anew in the heart of every reader.

Stanley Barnes
Hillsborough, 1998

"Goodbye, God"

❖

"Then said his wife unto him, Dost thou still retain thine integrity?
curse God and die. *But he said unto her, Thou speakest as one of*
the foolish women speaketh. What? shall we receive good at
the hand of God, and shall we not receive evil? In all this did not
Job sin with his lips." Job 2: 9,10

The word "curse" in the original means "bid farewell," or say "Goodbye to God." This is exactly what Satan said to God that Job would do. "Then Satan answered the Lord and said, Dost Job fear God for nought? Hast not Thou made a hedge about him, and about his house, and about all he hath on every side? Thou hast blessed the work of his hands, and his substance is increased in the land. **But** put forth Thine hand now, and touch all that he hath, and he will **curse** (say goodbye) Thee to Thy face." God gave him permission to touch all that he had. God could trust Job in adversity as well as prosperity. I wonder how many of us He could trust? God felt confident Job would not let Him down. Satan went out from God's presence to do his dirty work, but remember, he was under God's permission and supervision. He could only do what God permitted and no more. But what a calamity that was, **and all in one day**. 7000 sheep, 3000 camels, 8000 oxen, 500 asses, and last of all and sorest of all, seven sons and three daughters. What a day and what a calamity! Surely enough to provoke any man to say, "Goodbye to God." But what did Job do and say?

"Then Job arose and rent his mantle and shaved his head, and fell down upon the ground, **and worshipped**." (He didn't curse God, or complain or grumble, as many of us have done under far less trying conditions, and sad to say, as many are doing today) "And said, Naked came I out of my mother's womb, and naked shall I return thither: the Lord gave, and the Lord hath taken away; blessed be the name of the Lord. In all this Job sinned not, nor charged God foolishly."

Hallelujah! How pleased God must have been and how chagrined the old devil must have been.

JOB'S SECOND TEST

But in spite of this, Satan wouldn't acknowledge defeat, or cease from his tormenting Job, or agree with God's estimate of Job, that he was a perfect and upright man, one that feareth God and escheweth evil, **none like him in the earth**. So he answered the Lord and said, "Skin for skin, yea, all that a man hath will he give for his life. But put forth Thine hand now and touch his bone and his flesh and he will **curse** Thee (ie., say "Goodbye, God") to Thy face." God gave him permission again to test poor Job. "So Satan went forth from the presence of the Lord, and smote Job with sore boils, from the sole of his foot unto the crown" - the worst form of leprosy - horrible - loathsome. **Then** said his **wife** unto him, "Dost thou still retain thine integrity? Curse God and die." His wife entered, maybe unknowingly, into an alliance with Satan to make her husband curse God. She who of all on earth was his nearest and dearest, the bride of his youth, the mother of his seven noble sons and three fair daughters, now dead - the companion of his joys and sorrows. Beyond question, it was politic to attack Job through his wife, and probably for this reason she was spared, not because having her was a greater trial to the good man than losing her would have been, but because the devil wanted a tool against her husband. Chrysostom asks, "Why did the devil leave him his wife? Because he thought her a good scourge by which to plague him more acutely than by any other means." Temptation which comes through one whom we love is most powerful. This is a favourite way of the devil. He got Eve to tempt Adam and succeeded. In Job's case he failed.

DON'T JUDGE HIS WIFE TOO SEVERELY

Don't let us judge Job's wife too harshly. She never complained when her ten children were killed in one day. Not a murmur when her husband lost all his wealth and property. She could and did stand all that and not curse God or urge her husband to do so. But when she saw her husband smitten with such a foul and loathsome disease and knew what a good godly, God-fearing man he was, her confidence in God broke. She couldn't believe in a good, kind and loving God who would allow such loss and affliction to come upon him. Remember, she nor Job knew about the controversy God and Satan had. If she had only known that, I believe she would have held fast her confidence, but knowing nothing about it, she felt God wasn't dealing fair with her good and righteous husband. So she said, "What's the good? Who would serve such a cruel God?" And she urged Job to say, "Goodbye God." Could you blame her? What would we have done under similar aggravating circumstances?

WHERE IT HAPPENED

We must remember all this happened in Ur of the Chaldees - a heathen country. Job was a contemporary of Abram. Whether they ever met or knew each other, we have no record. It happened 600 years after the flood and 1800 years before Christ. Job was 60 years of age at the time. They hadn't the light that we have, 1900 years after Christ. God wasn't revealed as clearly and fully then as He is to us today. Yet in spite of the dim light he had and the meagre knowledge of God, Satan couldn't get him to say "Goodbye God," and neither could his wife, dear and all as she was to him. He said unto her, "Thou speakest as one of the **foolish** women speaketh. What? shall we receive good at the hand of God and shall we not receive evil?" No wonder God boasted about His servant. Listen! "The Lord said unto Satan, Hast thou **'considered'** my servant Job, **that there is none like him in the earth**, a perfect and upright man, one that feareth God and escheweth evil?" I wonder what the Lord's estimate of you and me is? Could He say about us what He said about Job? Can the Lord depend on you? Does He find you ever true? I believe that many of our trials and adversities are allowed to come to us, through Satan or Satan's emissaries, to see whether we serve God for nought. I wonder if we enable God to say about us, "There is none like him in the earth," or do we give the devil the chance of saying we will curse God to His face?

SCRIPTURE ILLUSTRATIONS

We find in Scripture instances of great men who let God down under trying circumstances. The vessel was marred. The trial revealed the weakness. For example, Abram was promised a son and waited 20 years and no sign or hope of one coming, so he and his wife determined to fulfil God's promise. Ishmael was the result. Moses lost his temper under the stress and strain of circumstances. Elijah could face 400 false prophets and a backsliding nation. He rang true to God; but when Jezebel threatened him, he went for his life like any coward. David could face lions, giants and armies, but failed before his lusts and gave God's enemies a chance to slander God. Jeremiah charged God with folly when he said, "Ah, Lord God! surely Thou hast greatly deceived this people and Jerusalem, saying, Ye shall have peace, whereas the sword reacheth into the soul." Listen to Jeremiah again, "I sat not in the assembly of the mockers, nor rejoiced. I sat alone because of Thy hand; for Thou hast filled me with indignation. Why is my pain perpetual and my wound incurable, which refuseth to be healed? Wilt Thou be altogether unto me as **a liar** and as waters that fail? Imagine calling God a liar because of some sickness unhealed. That would delight Satan and grieve God. John Baptist one day in prison called out "Art thou He that should come or look we for another?" These are a few samples of great and godly men who let God down when tested. They were men of like passions, as we are. When God writes their biographies He writes their failures as well as their successes. I wonder what He would write about us? I wonder would we be like Job, never charging God with folly or saying "Goodbye God," or would He have to record how we cried out like Jeremiah, "Wilt Thou be altogether unto me as **a liar?**" I have known those who have suffered long and severely and never charged God with folly or said "Goodbye God." I have known others who had some slight trouble or sickness and grumbled and complained and rebelled and charged God with folly yet never said "Goodbye God."

HOW HAVE WE ACTED?

Tell me, dear friend, when death entered your home and your love one was taken from you, did you worship or worry? Did you, by your murmuring and inconsolable grief, bid God goodbye?

How many have done that very thing? They have quit praying and reading their Bible. They rarely enter the church. They have given up all service for God. They felt that God had wronged them and dealt harshly with them, so they have said, "Goodbye God". Maybe you lost your job or business. Your money took wings. You were wrongly dealt with by others, maybe Christians. You tried to live for God and serve Him and yet in spite of it all, all this is allowed to come upon you. You were staggered. You were dumbfounded. You began to doubt God and then said to God, "Goodbye. If that's the way you treat those who love you and try to serve you, I'm through. Goodbye." Maybe, like Jeremiah, you cry out "Why is my pain perpetual and my wound incurable, which refuseth to be healed." You have been laid on a bed of pain and sickness for years. You have prayed and prayed and you have said, "Wilt Thou be altogether unto me as a liar or waters that fail?" You have become soured and cynical and unbelieving and have charged God foolishly. You see, dear friend, if you bid God goodbye, you **die**. Your hopes, your joy, your love, your faith, all die. You cannot evade or escape the consequences of your decision. Trust God even when you cannot understand and your love, joy, peace, faith and hope live. Say "Goodbye God," and all these precious fruits of the Spirit die. Friends, let us make up our minds that whatever our trials or sorrows may be, we will never say goodbye to God.

BIBLE EXHORTATION

We are told not to think it strange concerning the fiery trial. Jesus said, "In this world **ye shall have tribulation**." Paul tells us to "continue in the faith," and that "we must through much tribulation enter into the kingdom of God." We are to "consider Him that endured such contradiction of sinners against Himself, lest ye be wearied and faint in your minds. Ye have not yet resisted unto blood, striving against sin. And ye have forgotten the exhortation which speaketh unto you as unto children, My son despise not thou the chastening of the Lord, nor faint when thou art rebuked of Him; for whom the Lord loveth He chasteneth and scourgeth **every** son whom He receiveth. If ye endure chastening, God dealeth with you as with sons; for what son is he whom the father chasteneth not? But if ye be without chastisement, whereof **all** are partakers, then are ye bastards and not sons." I believe we often fail because we think no one has ever been tried just as we are or for such a long time. We forget that there is no trial but is common to **all** men. God never promised anyone a smooth passage. He does promise us a safe landing.

"God never would send you the darkness
If He thought you could bear the light,
But you would not cling to the guiding hand
If the way were always bright.
And you would not learn to walk by faith
Could you always walk by sight.

So He sends the blinding darkness
And the furnace of seven-fold heat,
'Tis the only way, believe me,
To keep you close to His feet.
For 'tis always so easy to wander
When our lives are glad and sweet.

Then nestle your hand in your Father's,
And sing, if you can, as you go,
Your song may cheer some one behind you
Whose courage is sinking low.
And well - if your lips do quiver -
God will love you the better so."

Suppose Job had let God down and obeyed his wife's advice and yielded to the devil, what a loss would have been ours. What a loss it would have been for him. The experience of Job has strengthened millions of fainting hearts and brought light to the perplexing problem of human suffering, and thus cheered sick, suffering and sorrowing pilgrims on their way. We are told that "Job sinned not nor charged God foolishly"; nor bid God "Goodbye." This is all merely negative.

JOB'S CONFIDENCE IN GOD

We also read his confession of his confidence in God. Listen! "Though he slay me, yet will I trust Him." There are many who would not dare to bid God goodbye or charge Him foolishly, but in their hearts they **sulk** and entertain an unpardonable feeling against God. They feel God has wronged them and dealt harshly with them. Their joy flies away. Their love dies. They continue professing to be a Christian and do some church work, but in their heart they hold a grudge against God. They cry out secretly, "Why? Why did God take my child? Why did my husband or wife die? Why should I have to suffer such pain?" etc., etc. Why be misunderstood or persecuted? Why? Why? Why? They move through a maze of interrogation marks. How different with Job. He confessed openly "Though He slay me yet will I trust Him." Let us compare our losses and trials, sickness and sorrows, with his, and it should make us ashamed and lead us to where we can and will openly confess it: "Though He slay me, yet will I trust Him."

OUR ENABLEMENT

We can do this easier and readier when we remember this word of God, "And we **know** - not **feel**, or **see**, or **understand** - No! - but **know** that **all things** - not **some things** - work together for good to them that love God, to them who are called according to His purpose." Tell me, friend, do you really love God? Are you able to say with Peter, "Thou knowest all things, Thou knowest that I love Thee." You may have some bother about your election and calling. Never mind. Do you really love God? Then be assured of this one unchanging and unchangeable **fact** - not **theory** - that all things work together for good, and only good. One version renders it: "God **is** - not **was** nor **will**, but **IS** - right now, and under present circumstances, working **all things** together for your good. Hallelujah! You may not see it, or think it, or feel it, but it is true none the less. Surely then in the light of such a revelation of God, you will confess, like Job, **openly** and **audibly**, "Though He slay me, yet will I trust him."

DO IT NOW

Do it, man, in spite of the devil, sickness, death, poverty, mysterious and tragic circumstances. Compel God to feel proud of you and be able to boast about you. One day we'll understand, when the mists have rolled away. All the trials and sorrows and sicknesses will seem as nothing when we stand before the Judgment seat of Christ and hear Him say, "Well done, good and faithful (not great and successful) servant, enter thou into the joy of Thy Lord." Never bid God "Goodbye" - never!

"God never does, nor suffers to be done,
But what thou would'st thyself,
Could'st thou but see
The end of all events as well as He."

The Necessity of Repentance

--- ❖ ---

"In those days came John the Baptist preaching in the wilderness of Judea, and saying, Repent ye." Matthew 3: 1-2

"From that time Jesus began to preach and to say, Repent." Matthew 4: 17

This isn't a very popular doctrine or word and rarely used today in our preaching. I wonder if this is the reason why there are so many 'nominal' or spurious Christians abounding. Whether popular or not it is Scriptural and necessary to our salvation. It was the theme of John's message and the beginning and end of Christ's.

I have often wondered why the word is rarely if ever used in our preaching and dealing with unsaved ones. There are various reasons given why this is so. Let us consider some of them.

THE WORD IS NOT USED IN THE GOSPEL OF JOHN

This is quite true, but then John's Gospel was not written about repentance, but about believing. The word "believe" is used over 90 times and all the sayings and miracles of Jesus were selected to illustrate and enforce this fact. Why should he bring in repentance? "These things were written that ye might believe." (John 20:31) The writers of the New Testament were logical and orderly in their writings. They didn't (like some preachers) try to drive several nails in at one time. Matthew wrote about the King; Mark about the servant; Luke about His humanity; and John about His Deity and our believing in Him.

THEY ALSO SAY IT WAS USED TO JEWS ALONE

They build this objection on Acts 5:31 - "Him hath God exalted with His right hand to be a Prince and a Saviour, for to give repentance to Israel." If these were the only words used then they would be justified in their objection. That is the danger we are all in when handling Scripture. We isolate words or passages from all other references and end up with the wildest notions and errors. Let us see other references. (Acts 11:18) - "When they heard these things they held their peace and glorified God, saying, Then hath God also to the Gentiles granted repentance unto life." We see from these words that repentance was not only for Jews but Gentiles. Another reference: (Acts 17:30) - "And the times of this ignorance God winked at, but now commandeth ALL men everywhere to repent." When are we to repent? Now. Who are to repent? All men. Where, or what country or dispensation? Everywhere. It is also the command of God.

THEY SAY IT IS LEGAL AND NOT GOSPEL

This reason is also strangely erroneous and unscriptural. Repentance is of Gospel origin and not legal, because Jesus preached it and not Moses. Then it is gracious in its origin, because it is the gift of God.

There is a two-fold danger we are likely to fall into if we are not careful.

1. We may make too little of Repentance.

We may under-rate, or may even dislike it. Am I right in saying "repentance" is the most unpopular word in the whole vocabulary of religion? Has not every sinner a strong prejudice against repentance? Is it not so, that men would rather hear of anything else than repentance? It is utterly repugnant and repulsive to the carnal, unsanctified Christian. He desires and demands forgiveness without any qualification on his part whatever. If this is so with the unsanctified believer, how much more is it so with the unsaved sinner. Whether popular or unpopular, it is the immutable Word of God. It is mentioned 100 times in the Bible. It is used 58 times in the New Testament; of these 25 are to be ascribed to Luke in his Gospel and the Acts, and twelve of the Apocalypse. St Paul uses it five times. Would God command us to repent, and offer it to us if it were unimportant or non-essential? Salvation then cannot be without repentance, anymore than without faith. If I can reconcile any to "the sweet grace" of repentance, and lead you to say with Bengel, "Repentance is a joyful gift and not a matter of sorrow"; and to think of repentance as did one of the old Puritans, who said, "I should like to die repenting"; this article and labour of love will not have been in vain. Remember, we don't bring repentance to Christ but get repentance from Christ.

2. We may make too much of Repentance.

The sinner who says or thinks, "I have not repented enough, I don't feel my sins enough, I am waiting for deeper feelings" is making too much of repentance. He is trusting to repentance instead of to Christ. He is putting his tears in the place of Christ's blood.

"It is not thy tears of repentance or prayers,
But the blood that atones for the soul,
On Him then who shed it thou may'st at once
Thy weight of iniquities roll."

A sense of sin in the prodigal son was good, but only so far as it led him home. A sense of sin with the sinner is useful - good - only if it leads you to quicken your steps to Jesus Christ for forgiveness and salvation.

Therefore let us be warned concerning this two-fold danger regarding repentance, and give it its rightful and God-appointed place in our salvation. Repentance does not renew the heart; this can only be effected by regenerating grace; neither is repentance the same in all its circumstances in every individual. There appears to have been as much difference between the repentance of Lydia and the jailor as between the outward circumstances under which they respectively received repenting grace; the one by the side of a sweetly flowing river, the other amidst a scene of the utmost consternation and terror. It isn't a question of "how" or "how much" we have repented, but have we repented of our sins, and do we enjoy the experience of continued repentance? Let us see the necessity for it if we are to be saved, and give it the important place given to it in the Word of God.

It was the theme of Old Testament prophets. John the Baptist began and continued his ministry with it. Jesus took it for His first message, and He also gave it as His last message after His death and resurrection. It was the burden of Peter's message at Pentecost. When they cried, "Men and brethren, what shall we do?" Peter said "Repent." (Acts 2:38) When Paul was defending himself and preaching before the Ephesian elders he said he "testified both to the Jews and also to the Greeks 'repentance' toward God and faith toward our Lord Jesus Christ." When he stood before Agrippa on his defence he said, "O King Agrippa, I was not disobedient unto the heavenly vision, but shewed first unto them at Damascus and at Jerusalem and throughout all the coasts of Judea, and then to the Gentiles that they should 'repent' and turn to God and do works meet for repentance." And because he preached this unpopular doctrine, the Jews caught him in the temple and went about to kill him. (Acts 26:19-21) It wasn't popular then, and is not popular today. But popular or not it is the Word of God, and if we don't repent we shall surely perish.

True repentance, or repentance unto life, may be summed up in these words: The conviction of the presence of all evil and the absence of all good. Where there is true repentance there never is and never can be smug complacency and self-righteous contentment. If we have a good thing to say about ourselves or our so-called good works, there is no true repentance in the heart. Every true repentant and repenting believer feels with the Apostle Paul that he is "the chief of sinners."

The old Puritan said that he had no quarrel with what Paul said when he said he was the chief of sinners, but he did quarrel with him for taking his place. So every true penitent feels the same, in some measure about it. Paul said there was no good thing in his flesh, but that he was incorrigible, "was not subject to the law of God, and neither indeed could be," and could never please God. Never mind what our definition of repentance may be, let us be sure of this one thing, that there is no repentance unto life - true repentance - where we deny or do not feel utterly sinful and vile, and never can be anything else, apart from His saving grace. These are days when original sin and total depravity are denied or disdained and treated as if it was some antiquated and antedated bogey. We are deifying humanity and humanizing Deity, and making Christ's death on Calvary anything else or something less than a substitutionary sacrifice for our sin and us sinners.

True repentance - repentance unto life - is intellectual, emotional, and volitional. That is, it is a change of mind, a change of feeling, a change of purpose. Let us consider each of these separately and carefully.

1. A CHANGE OF MIND. (INTELLECTUAL)

It is a change of mind concerning three things.

(i) Concerning God.

We find that God's love is not in conflict with His wrath; nor His mercy inconsistent with His justice. The unrepentant sinner is wrong concerning God's love and God's wrath. He either believes He is all love and no justice or wrath, or all wrath and no mercy or love. But in repentance he comes to see that God can be just and yet justify the ungodly sinner. He also realises that salvation isn't God making light of sin or overlooking it, but that he has given His well beloved and only begotten Son to be the sinner's substitute and the sacrifice for his sin. "Jesus paid it all, all to Him I owe," is his song. An old Scots woman was dying. She was asked if God's love gave her any comfort. "Oh, no," she said, "I have never deserved it." Was it His mercy? "No, I have never had any right to it." They were amazed, and asked her, What is it, then, gives you such peace and comfort in your dying hour? She said, "It is His righteousness. He has given me His word that if I believed in Jesus as my Saviour, He would give me eternal life and I'd never perish. He is righteous and can never break His word."

(ii) Concerning Sin.

The unrepentant sinner revels in sin, makes a mock of sin,

lives in sin, delights in sin; but when he receives the gift of repentance, he begins to fear sin, to dread sin, and abhor sin. Sin becomes an awful reality, and he feels hell should be his portion for ever on account of his sin. He ceases to laugh at sin or make excuse for it. He longs to be delivered from the guilt and bondage of it. His conscience begins to ache like a naked nerve in a tooth. He feels he is "the" (not a) chief of sinners. He begins to wonder whether such a sinner as he could ever be saved and justified. All his self-righteousness and self and smug complacency feels like filthy rags and a body of death, and he continually cries out, "O wretched man that I am." He counts, like Paul, all his good works and church connection and sacraments and good living, as "dung". He loathes them as much as his sin, and longs to be free and at peace.

(iii) Concerning himself.

What a marvellous change comes over the sinner who truly repents concerning himself. Before he began to repent he was thoroughly convinced that he was as good as the best, if not a little better. He could plume himself like a peacock before God and man, and even thank God he was not like other men. He felt and said, if he didn't get to heaven, he didn't know who would. Didn't he pay twenty shillings in the pound and observe the golden rule and follow the light of his conscience and do all the good he could. Didn't he belong to church and attend it regularly and give generously? What more could either God or man require? What a change when God gives him true repentance. How he loathes himself; how he despises himself. His "righteousnesses," not his wickednesses, become loathsome, filthy rags.

Like Job he repents in dust and ashes. He feels he is unfit for the society of men, let alone the service of God. Oh, how he mourns over his sin and sinfulness, and lashes his conscience because he ever said and thought he was righteous and deserving. Remember that this loathing and lashing of conscience on account of sin, isn't the experience of a real deep-dyed sinner. He usually feels this way after conversion, not before, because his moral sense has been blunted and seared by his wild life and sinning. But those who have lived naturally moral and pure upright lives, when they are given repentance they are more sensitive in conscience and suffer accordingly.

In true repentance we truly change our mind concerning sin and self. We see them in their true and awful nature and begin to feel as God feels towards them.

2. IT IS ALSO A CHANGE OF FEELING. (EMOTIONAL)

The sinner begins to sorrow - to feel sorry - for his sins. His sorrow is such that he begins to hate it. Tears and groans are not strangers to him. Once he found pleasure in it; once it was his delight. Now it is the cause and source of all his grief and sorrow. All feeling of smug complacency has vanished like the morning cloud and early dew. I believe the reason for so many spurious conversions and shallow, superficial Christian living is a spurious repentance, or lack of repentance. When there is true, God-given repentance, there will always be sincere grief for sin and sincere hatred of sin. O what a change of feeling in the truly repentant. He used to live in sin, now he longs to be delivered from it. He used to love sin, now he loathes it. He used to revel in sin, now he runs from it. He used to delight in sin, now he detests it. Hatred of sin is not genuine if it is not universal and irreconcilable - universal (against all sin), and irreconcilable to any known sin.

3. IT IS ALSO A CHANGE OF PURPOSE. (VOLITIONAL)

The whole trend and course of his life is changed. True repentance always leads to a turning away from sin unto God, with full purpose of and endeavour after a new obedience. This is what completes repentance not to be repented of. And it consists chiefly in this; for it is this that evidences that sin is the object of our grief and hatred. Turning from sin implies a turning from **all** sin, both in heart and life. A turning away from sin and a resistance of its outbreakings, a turning from the sin that most easily besets us; a turning from all temptations to sin; a watching against all   occasions of sin, from a conviction that unwatchfulness is sinful in itself and accompanied with the worst of consequences. Full purpose of new obedience implies that the true penitent resolves to turn immediately to the practice of every known duty required of him by his Lord and Saviour, and that he will serve Him in spirit and in truth. But this is not all. There must be some   evidence that the sinner acts according to his purpose - there must be an endeavour after new obedience. It is **new** obedience because it proceeds from new principles, it is influenced by new motives, and it is performed in a new manner. Formerly the   sinner trusted in his own strength to perform obedience; now he does all in the strength of Christ. It is directed to a new end - the glory of God. We not only sorrow for sin, but we cease from it and seek to serve God.

True repentance is wrought in the heart of the sinner by the Spirit of God. That man cannot produce in himself that godly sorrow which is not to be repented of, is evident from Jeremiah 13: 23 - "Can the Ethiopian change his skin or the leopard his spots." In like manner it is impossible for a sinner to turn himself from sin unto God. It is true that a man may depart from gross sins, but the Holy Spirit alone can turn the heart from sin. His power alone can sanctify and keep us pure within. It is not of works or the will of man, but purely of grace lest any should boast.

The means used by the Spirit to produce this work of grace in the heart of the sinner is the Word of God. It comes as a hammer to break in pieces the hard and stony heart. It thunders out the law and our guilt and condemnation, but it is also the Gospel - the good news, that "God so loved the world that He gave His only begotten Son that whosoever believeth in Him should not perish but have everlasting life." It is the Gospel that is "the power of God unto salvation to everyone that believeth." If this does not prove effectual for the purposes of salvation, nothing else will.

Let us consider from real life how the Holy Spirit produced this sweet grace in the lives of men in the Bible.

DAVID

David said, "I thought on my ways and turned." As he seriously thought the Spirit of God led him to repentance. He thought about his sin and sinning, about God's love and mercy, and this led him to sorrow for and cease from sin and turn to God.

THE PRODIGAL

The prodigal son was led to repent through the failure of his life. He left home and father and started out for the far country and a good time. He had a good time for a while, but it soon ended, and he finished up at the swine trough, feeding pigs, hungry and lonely, forsaken by all his friends.

The Holy Spirit used these very circumstances to produce true repentance, and he came home. What a welcome! His father kissed him before even he washed his face.

This has been the means used by the Spirit in many cases since. It was this that broke my heart and led me home to Christ. As a young man I left home and loved ones. Tired of piety and family prayers I set out to have a good time. I certainly had a good time too, but never truly satisfied, and the good time was transient and intermittent, until at last, disgusted and disappointed with it all, I saw what a failure I was making of my life. My ideas and ambitions were blighted, my heart was dissatisfied and discontented, my hopes were ruined. This all led home, and soon after to the Saviour. How often the Spirit uses this sense of failure to produce repentance and lead to Christ.

PENTECOST

While Peter preached to the crowds in Jerusalem at Pentecost, 3000 and 5000 were led to repent and believe. The word of condemnation and salvation was used by the Spirit in a wonderful way that day. That is why we should try and bring sinners to hear the Word of God, while they listen the Holy Spirit produces repentance. The old devil will move earth and hell to hinder Christians from inviting sinners to the services and prevent the sinners from attending. Well he knows the means used by the Spirit to produce true repentance in the sinner.

THE JAILOR

The Philippian Jailor was a hard-hearted careless sinner. No doubt a good Government servant. All the preaching, singing and testimony of the Apostles never moved him, so God sent an earthquake to shake fear into him and shake the indifference out of him. This was the means used by the Spirit to produce repentance in this hard-hearted jailor. He often uses God's providences in our lives, since we go along through life careless and indifferent, no thought of God or our soul, its peril and danger and need of salvation. God sends some sorrow or calamity to shake us out of our careless indifference. A child dies. A loved one dearer than life itself is taken from us. Our money takes wings and flies away. We fail in business or lose our job. Sickness overtakes us and we are laid aside in pain and weakness. Our will bends, our heart breaks, and we are led to true repentance. Thank God for His providences that were used by the Spirit to produce true repentance in us. Whatever means He may use to lead us to repentance, let us bless Him for them. Let us remember He has many ways of producing it, and let us not limit Him in His working in the lives of our loved ones.

Just one more word that might help some one. With respect to the order of faith and repentance, we may hear remark that in respect to time, all the blessings of salvation are bestowed at once, but in the order of nature, faith must precede repentance. This is evident from the nature of repentance itself. Repentance is a turning from sin to God, but there can be no turning to God but through Christ, and there can be no coming to Christ but by faith. There is no need to argue which is first, it would be like arguing which spoke in a wheel turned first when the wheel moved. But let us see to this, if we do not repent we will surely perish eternally. **Repent or perish**. Let me quote the Shorter Catechism: "Repentance unto life is a saving grace, whereby a sinner out of a true sense of his sin, and apprehension of the mercy of God in Christ, doth with grief and hatred of sin, turn from it unto God, with full purpose of and endeavour after new obedience."

Regeneration

❖

"Marvel not that I say unto thee, Ye must be born again."
John 3: 7

There are two outstanding characteristics regarding Christianity that are never called in question today by any thinking man or woman:-

First - That in the PERSON of Jesus Christ, Christianity has given to the world the most perfect human life it has ever seen. It is very significant. It does not matter whether the man is a believer in Christ or not, when they mention Him in their writings or speeches, they are all united in this one fact, that no other religion known has ever given to the world such a being. There is no comparison between Christ and the founders of other religions. If you try to compare them it is like comparing a candle to the sun. HE is the Incomparable Christ.

Second - That in the TEACHING of Jesus Christ, Christianity has given to the world the most perfect ethical code it has ever known. That is, in Jesus Christ, we have the only perfect pattern of human life, and in the Teaching of Jesus Christ, we have the only perfect teaching. All agree - infidels or believers - that if we could live as He lived and do as He taught, the golden age would dawn on this old world. But that is just where the difficulty comes in. "IF" we could live as He lived and as he taught. There has never been a man who lived as He lived or did as He taught, at any time, any place, and there never will be. So if Jesus only came to this world to be an example of a perfect human life, and a teacher, He has only come to mock poor, helpless, ruined humanity in its helpless, hopeless condition. For while we can admire and do admire His life and all He taught, we know that we can never hope to be like Him, or obey His teaching, as we ought.

CHRIST MORE THAN AN EXAMPLE

So Christianity is not merely a perfect life presented. It is not merely a perfect ethical code enunciated, but it is essentially and supremely a divine life communicated. "Ye must be born again" if ye would enter the kingdom of heaven. There is no other subject so unpopular in the world today as this, "Ye must be born again." There are those who deny it altogether, and believe they can, and will, enter heaven by their own natural goodness and good works. They won't have anything to do with the doctrine of total depravity. They think it is a slight on humanity. They think that there is something good in man, and all they need is to develop it. They won't believe that their righteousnesses are filthy rags in the sight of God. What must their worst be like in His sight? Dear friends, God has made it plain that our righteousness will never gain us an entrance into heaven. Others accept the doctrine of total depravity, but make light of its clear meaning and teaching by saying "it isn't a new creation, but the redirection of existing faculties, etc." That is, all man needs is better teaching and better environment, and he will be fit for God and heaven. Others, again, believe it, but it is for others, not for themselves. They imagine because they have been well born and are now well behaved and have been all their life - they are very amiable, generous, kind, good church workers, regular attenders of the church, they are always at Communion, they never eat beef on Fridays, but always fish, and they keep Lent faithfully and pray or SAY their prayers regularly - that they are exempt from this "being born again." Drunkards and ignorant vile sinners need to be born again, but then they are not like that, and therefore it is not for them.

NICODEMUS

When you hear them talk like this, you would almost imagine that these words were uttered by the Lord to some great outstanding sinner, but instead of that they were uttered to a very religious man, and I suppose if ever there was a man who wore the white flower of a blameless life it was this man, and yet Jesus said to him, "YE must be born again." Could you say you are either as good or as religious as he was? Jesus didn't say these words to the woman of Samaria or Mary Magdalene, but to the Principal of the Theological College in Jerusalem, and the leading member of the Sanhedrin. If he needed to be born again to enter the kingdom of heaven, do you think that you will get into it any other way? But even if you were better in every way than Nicodemus was, still you MUST be born again if you would enter the kingdom of heaven. His religious creed wasn't sufficient, his membership of the Sanhedrin, his performance of religious duties, his high moral character and his acknowledgment of Jesus Christ as sent from God, were not sufficient. If ever he was either to see or enter the kingdom of God he must be born again, and so must you.

FOUR THINGS

There are FOUR things I would like to say about being "Born Again":-

First - It is a **universal need**. It doesn't matter who you are or what you are, or where you live or what your believe, "You must be born again." You may be black or white, red or yellow, in your skin; you must be born again. You may be rich or poor, you may be a mendicant or a millionaire; you must be born again. You may be a drunkard or a temperate man, good or bad, virtuous or vicious, honest or dishonest, educated or ignorant. It doesn't matter what you are or how you live or look, "Ye must be born again". God is no respecter of persons. We are apt to think that people, because they are nice, and come of a good family and live decent and are religious, that they are all right for Heaven. Ah no, friend, there are a lot of well educated, well behaved, baptised, religious people in hell today. There are many there who were far better in their lives and did more for the world than ever you have done, but they are damned because, like you, they would not believe they needed to be born again. You may be a very zealous Episcopalian or a very orthodox Presbyterian or even a red-hot Methodist or a strong believer in immersion, or even a determined Plymouth Brother, and think that, because you have come out from amongst all these other denominations and you meet in your own wee room or hall, that you are exempt. No, no, ALL must be born again. It doesn't matter what your creed or character is, "Ye must be born again."

NO DIFFERENCE

There is no difference with God. Man, do you think that God will change this word of His to suit you and gain you as a subject for His kingdom? You surely have a very high estimation of your own importance and a very low conception of the Lord. If you want to become a citizen of the kingdom of heaven and a subject of King Jesus, then this is the only way, "Ye must be born again." If you want to become a citizen of the United States of America, you have to take an oath something like this: "I swear and abjure all fidelity and allegiance to every foreign prince, potentate and power, etc." Could you imagine a man saying to the Judge: "Judge, this oath is too strong, but if you will alter it a little to suit me, then I'll take it and become a citizen of this country." Do you think that it would be changed to suit you? Man, what sort of a country would it become if it was changed to suit every man who didn't like it. Do you imagine that God hasn't as much sense in this matter about His kingdom as Uncle Sam has about his Republic? If a man wants to become a Freemason or an Orangeman he would have to take the oath and adhere to the constitution of the order, wouldn't he? Is it altered for every man desiring to join, but who doesn't care for the oath or the constitution? Certainly it isn't. What sort of an order would it become if such were the case?

GIVE GOD A CHANCE

Well, I say, folks, don't you think God has just about as much sense regarding becoming a citizen of His kingdom? Certainly He has. God will never change it to suit you or anybody else. Give God the same liberty and right as we demand for our country and lodges. Dear me, what impertinence on the part of any man to try and get God to alter this law of His merely to gain you or others like you. There is something far more important to God than getting you saved, and that is His own integrity. He will never sacrifice that to gain you or a million like you. "Ye must be born again." Isn't it His kingdom? Hasn't He the right to say who are to be there and how they are to enter? If He gave us our desserts he would damn us in hell; for that is what we deserve. He is under no obligation to any of us. There are no exceptions. "YE" must be born again if ye would enter the kingdom of heaven. It includes you and everybody else. Don't exclude yourself and damn your own soul.

Second - It is **an absolute necessity**. "Ye MUST be born again." Not "Ye MAY be born again," but Ye MUST. I used to have the idea that God, being an Autocratic Sovereign, could just do as He liked, and that one day he took a notion that the only way men and women could get to heaven was to be born again. But do you know, the more I have thought about it, the more convinced am I of the wisdom and love of God in making it imperative that we must be born again if we would enter the kingdom of heaven. Just think! If the Lord took you to heaven, just as you are by nature - nice, kind, good, amiable, generous, religious, church member; baptised, catechised, confirmed communicant - it would be a million times greater torment than the lowest hell.

A CRUEL MONSTER

God would be nothing but a cruel monster if He did a thing like that to you. Could you imagine a more cruel act on the part of any man than taking a hen and putting it in the water and trying to make it live like a fish, or taking a fish and trying to make it live on land like a hen. It would be monstrous, and in this civilised land it would not be permitted. Such an act as that would be severely punished. Do you think for a moment that God would be so cruel to you. The only way you could make a hen live like a fish would be to perform a miracle on it and take the lungs out of it and put gills in it, or to make a fish live like a hen you would have to take the gills out of it and put lungs in it. It is just as big a miracle, and bigger, for God to make the natural man fit for heaven. He has to perform the most wonderful miracle on him by regenerating him - by being born again - making him entirely a new creation altogether. Yes, it is the love and wisdom of God that compels Him to say, "Ye must be born again if ye would enter the kingdom of heaven." Your condition by nature makes it imperative for you to be born again. What would you do in heaven? The very thought of holiness or the presence of holy people is very repugnant to you. You feel you are out of your element altogether. To spend an hour in prayer or half a night in prayer or at a prayer meeting would be refined torment to you. It takes you all your time to put up with an hour or two once a week in church, and then you take care that the service is not of an alarming sort. It is with a sigh of relief you leave the church when it is all over, and you say, "Well that is over for another week, thank God." What on earth would you do in heaven? Whatever you have of religion is a sort of painful religious duty. You have neither joy nor delight in it. You could almost wish that civilisation would not make such demands of you. You want to be thought decent in the eyes of society, and so you go to church and make some profession and pretence of religion. My! how you do enjoy a dance or an opera or a picture show or some other form of amusement.

YOUR LIFE

These things are life to you, but the Lord and the things of the Lord and your soul's eternal welfare are mere necessary nuisances that you have to put up with. A novel is such a delight to you, but the Word of God is a strange and uninteresting book to you. Now, seeing this is all so, tell me, friend, what on earth would you do if you went to heaven? What pleasure would you have there? What would there be that would interest you or that you would feel you were at home with? Don't you realise that it is the wisdom and love and mercy of God that commands you to be born again. You would just be about as much out of place there as the hen would be if it was put in the water to live or the fish put on the land to live like a hen. They would be out of their element altogether, and so would you if you got to heaven without being born again. "Ye must be born again if ye would enter the kingdom of heaven."

NO SUBSTITUTE

You can never successfully substitute anything else for this. You may try baptism, confirmation, church membership, good living, honest efforts to live as best you can, education, doing all the good you can for others. It will all fail, for "that which is born of the flesh is flesh" and nothing but flesh, and always will be flesh, and "flesh and blood can never enter the kingdom of heaven." It may become religious flesh, or educated flesh, or decent flesh, or drunken flesh, but it will always be nothing else but flesh. It doesn't matter what you do with it, you can never change its nature. You can train a wee pig to do all sorts of tricks and to live very clean and decent, but after you have spent all the time and effort and maybe money on its training, you haven't changed in one particle its nature; it is still a pig. So it is with the natural man. You can't change him by any or all of the things that are being tried today. You may cultivate and domesticate an acorn, but it will always become an oak tree. You can bend it or straighten it, you can weaken or strengthen it, but you can never change its nature. It will always be an oak. I remember being in a beautiful conservatory once and seeing a most beautiful plant. It was coloured so beautifully, I wondered what it was. My friend told me to feel it and I would soon find out what it was. I did so, and found out by its sting that it was just a common nettle, but it had been cultivated very carefully and expensively. They had succeeded in changing its looks, but they hadn't changed its nature. So it is with your nature and mine. It can never be changed. You can make it look nice and act nice, but it is still the same old God-hating thing. If we are to be fit for service here and heaven hereafter, we MUST be born again.

GOD STRANGE

God would be acting very strange if he was different in the spiritual realm from what He is in the natural. When you plant potatoes you get potatoes, you don't get turnips or carrots. When you sow wheat you get a harvest of wheat. You don't get barley or corn. My! what sort of a world would it be if, when we sowed our seed, we were never sure what sort of a crop we would get? You reap what you sow. That is just as true in the natural man. We are born of corruptible seed and our offspring is corrupt. You wouldn't expect it to be anything else, would you. You never heard or read of a cow bringing forth a horse or a dog. No, they only bear calves. Everything after its own kind, said God, at the beginning. It is just the same today. Sinners only and always bring forth sinners with natures so depraved and deceitful that there is no hope for them, unless they are born again.

AN EXCEPTION

I was saying there is no exception to this rule. But there is. There is a class of people who do not need to be born again. Those who don't want to go to heaven. The devil will take you as you are. He doesn't care whether you have been baptised, catechised or confirmed; whether you are a church member or not; whether you are good or bad, drunk or sober, educated or ignorant, rich or poor. It doesn't matter to him at all, as long as you let him get you to hell. This is the only class who are excepted - the people who don't want to go to heaven. But if you would enter the kingdom of heaven you MUST be born again. Now make no mistake about his, for it is fatal. There is a fixed gulf between the mineral kingdom and the vegetable, between the animal kingdom and the human. You cannot bridge it over. So there is a fixed gulf between the natural kingdom and the spiritual. It cannot be bridged over by any human invention. It can only be done by the Lord. When we come to Him and believe on Him, that gulf is bridged, and we are translated out of the kingdom of darkness into the kingdom of His dear Son. You may teach a blind man how to mix colours, but all the knowledge you impart to him will never give him his sight. He may be able to lecture with eloquence and learning, but he still remains blind. You can take a poor boy and teach him how to act and talk like a king, but you cannot make him a king. Kings are born, not made.

STONES NOT BRICKS

The Lord never says in His Word that we are BRICKS. No. But He does say we are STONES. Man makes bricks, but man never made a stone. God makes them. There are too many BRICK Christians in the Church today, and not enough living stones. You may educate a child in all the ways of Christianity so that it will become proficient, but after all is done and said, you haven't made a Christian out of it. "Ye MUST be born again." Surely you see, dear friends, how imperative it is. "Ye MUST be born again." I have almost exhausted your patience with my reiteration of this solemn fact. I have done so because you will never see the kingdom of heaven unless you are born again, and I know you want to be in heaven as I do myself, and we all do. Well, don't let the devil deceive you and damn you by some false notion or way.

Third - It is a **mystery unfathomable**. You cannot understand or explain it. When Nicodemus said, "How can these things be?" the Lord didn't cater to his curiosity in the matter, but He just said, "The wind bloweth where it listeth, and thou hearest the sound thereof, but canst not tell when it cometh or whither it goeth; so is everyone that is born of the Spirit."

NOT CREDULITY

But, mind you, although we cannot understand it, yet, we are not credulous, for the Lord said also, "Verily, verily, I say unto you. We speak that we do know, and testify that we have seen." I can imagine you saying, "Do you believe what you don't or cannot understand?" Certainly we do, and so do you, unless you are a fool. What is there you cannot understand and yet you believe? Can you understand the wind? Have you ever seen it? Have you ever tasted it? No. Yet you believe there is such a thing. I have sailed for months by the wind and never saw it, and couldn't tell whence it came or whither it went, but we trimmed our sails and we were carried along. Did you ever see a child grow? Yet you believe it grows. Can you understand it? Yet you believe it. How is it you can get fresh fish out of salt water? If you put a fish in salt water it will get salt. Do you believe you get fresh fish out of salt water? Certainly you do - and still you cannot understand it. Man, you are fit for the asylum if you won't believe what you cannot understand. Can you understand how of where sensations becomes consciousness? I feel with my fingers or taste with my tongue. Where does this feeling change into consciousness? You can't tell, nor anyone else, yet you and they believe in such a thing. You couldn't do otherwise. Do you understand electricity? Is it fluid or energy? Does it run along the wires or in the wires? What is it? You can't tell, but you believe in it.

MINISTER AND DOCTOR

A minister was preaching one Sunday in his church in a country village. The local doctor used to come in now and then, just to patronise the minister. They used to sit and chat together at times after the services of the Sunday were over. This Sunday evening the minister was preaching on "Ye must be born again." Among other things he said was this, "He couldn't understand being born again, although he believed it." After he got home the doctor called on him, and after some chatting the doctor said, "I was surprised at what you said tonight. I always thought you were a man of some intelligence. You said you believe in what you could not and did not understand." "That is true," said the minister. The doctor said, "How absurd. Did you ever see regeneration? No. Did you ever taste it? No. Did you ever smell it? No. Did you ever hear it? No. Did you ever feel it?" "Oh, yes, I have," said the minister. "Well," said the doctor, "will you believe what four out of five senses are against?" "Let me answer that," said the minister, "by asking you a question. Do you believe in pain?" "Certainly I do." "Have you ever seen it? No. Have you ever tasted it? No. Have you ever heard it? No. Have you ever smelled it? No. Have you ever felt it?" "Certainly I have." "Yet you believe in what four out of five of your senses are against." The doctor saw how absurd his position was. Your position is just as absurd as his, if you believe only what you can understand.

MYSTERIES

We are surrounded with mysteries. But we are forced to believe in them, though we cannot either explain them or understand them. You eat bread and butter, beef and potatoes. You drink tea and coffee, and water and milk. How is all this changed into bone, brain, blood, skin, hair, nails, teeth, sinew, nerve? Who can explain it? No one can. But we all believe it is a fact. A cow eats grass and gives milk. A horse eats grass and gives leather. A sheep eats grass and gives mutton and wool. A pig eats grass and gives pork. A hen eats it and lays eggs. Can you understand it? Certainly you can't, but yet you believe it. It is just the same about regeneration. We cannot understand it. It is a mystery, but on that account don't deny it or disbelieve it.

Fourth - It is **a glorious reality**. We know that we have passed out of death into life. Out of condemnation and guilt into freedom and pardon. We don't "hope" or "think" or "believe" or "trust". We KNOW. If you asked me, "Are you a married man?" I wouldn't say, "I hope I am, but I am doing my best." Oh no. It would be absurd. Still there are many, and this is the way they talk about being saved or being born again. You are either in the devil's family or in the Lord's. You are either a child of the devil or a child of God. You cannot be both at the same time, or half and half. When a man accepts the Lord Jesus as his Saviour He gives him the right to become a child of God. How do we know? We know, for sure, because we come to Jesus as guilty, lost, ruined, sinners, and accept Him as our own personal Saviour, and His Word assures us, and His Spirit witnesses with our spirit that we are born again. There are three things true about every one of us by nature. Our mind is darkened, our wills are rebellious, our affections are alienated. This was the result of the Fall. Adam lost the knowledge of God, then he hated God and rebelled against God, and this is true of every son of Adam today. But when we are born again, what happens? Our minds are illuminated and we get the light of the knowledge of the glory of God; our wills are subdued, so that we desire to know and endeavour to do the will of God; in fact, it is our delight, our affections are no longer alienated, for we love God with all our heart and strength. We cannot help it. Just as natural as a child loving its mother, we love God when we are born again.

A GLORIOUS REALITY

Oh! it is a glorious reality. Twenty-five years ago, sitting at my mother's fireside waiting for breakfast one Monday morning, between half-past eight and a quarter to nine o'clock, I accepted Jesus Christ as my personal Saviour, and immediately I was born again and knew it. I said to my mother, "Mother,

your prayers are answered and your anxiety is ended. I am saved."
Her joy was unspeakable and full of glory. Are we supposed to
believe our senses when they tell us about natural things, but
when they come to give evidence about spiritual things, then
they are liars? Such nonsense. And yet there are many who think
this is so. How do I know honey is sweet? I have tasted its sweet-
ness. How do I know fire burns? I have felt it burn. How do I
know that red is red, or black black, or green green? I have seen
it. How do I know one note of music from another? I have heard
them. How do I know a thing has an evil smell? Because I have
smelled it. Are we not to believe our senses? What can we
believe if we can't believe them? Are my senses not as depend-
able about spiritual things as they are about natural things? Certainly they are. I have seen the Lord. I have felt the Lord: I have
tasted - the Lord is good. "That which was from the beginning,
which we have heard, which we have seen with our eyes, which
we have looked upon, and our hands have handled of the Word
of Life," was John's way of putting it, and it is ours, too. We would
as soon doubt our own existence as doubt the reality of this fact
- we are born again.

A CHANGE

Then there is such a change wrought in the life of every born
again man. We are not what we ought to be or might be, but we
are not what we USED to be, and, glory to God! we are not what
we are going to be. We are at home in a prayer meeting. We
would feel very much out of place in a picture show or a theatre.
And yet there was a time when it was just the reverse. We love
the brethren; we love His Word. We delight to pray. We long to
win others to Christ. We love holiness, and hate sin. Our joys
are not in this life, but in the life to come. Like Paul, we say, "To
me to live is Christ, and to die is gain." Friend, if you have more
joy in a picture show than a prayer meeting, if you feel more at

home there than in a prayer meeting, you may make up your mind that you have never been born again. You may have made some sort of profession, but that is all. Your nature has never been changed. The sow may have been washed, and is therefore a clean sow - but just a SOW. The dog is turned to his own vomit again, but was never anything else but a dog. If we are born again, old things are passed away and all things become new. We would as soon doubt we were living as doubt we are born again, for the change is so evident in our lives. If there is no outward change, then, friend, you can make sure you have never been born again. The last logical argument to the man in the street that an apple tree is an apple tree is the apples it bears. By their fruits ye shall know them. Glory to God; there is no doubt about the reality of this matter. "By this we KNOW we are the children of God, when we love God and keep His commandments."

HOW IT HAPPENS

I trust there are some of you here, and you are asking in your mind and heart, "What must I do to be born again?" You say you have heard all about this again and again, but you seldom, if ever, heard how it is brought about. Our Lord hasn't left us in the dark about the matter. Nicodemus was puzzled about the same matter. He said, "How can a man be born when he is old?" Can he enter the second time into his mother's womb and be born?" Even if he could, it wouldn't make any difference. He would just be a sinner as much as ever. He wouldn't be one bit changed. Jesus took him back to the Old Testament story of the Israelites and the brazen serpent, and said, "As Moses lifted up the serpent in the wilderness, even so must the Son of Man be lifted up, that whosoever believeth or looketh on Him should not perish, but have eternal life." The serpent-bitten man was healed the moment he looked. It didn't make one particle of difference whether he was almost dead or only slightly bitten. The moment he looked he was healed. It is the very same with the sinner and Christ. Whether we are young or old, rich or poor, good or bad, Presbyterian or Episcopalian, Methodist or Baptist, we must look if we are to live, for -

> *"There is life for a LOOK at the Crucified One,*
> *There is life at this moment for thee,*
> *Then look, sinner, look unto Him and be saved,*
> *Unto Him who was nailed to the tree."*

HOW SIMPLE

Thank God for the simplicity of it all! I believe it is this that staggers many and keeps them back from the Lord. They think that some wonderful thing must be done or felt before they can be born again. No, it is just LOOK to Christ. You say, "Can the habits of a lifetime be changed by a look? Can a man's nature be changed as simply as this?" Glory to God! it can. Make the venture. Try it. Take our word for it. We have done it, and it works out all right. There is no risk with it. It is sure. It never fails. Millions are on the way to heaven, and this is what they did when they started. Millions are now in heaven, and this is what they did when they started. Surely you can believe their report and ours, if you feel that you cannot venture on the naked Word of God. Come, give Christ a chance. Remember, if you don't, you will never enter the kingdom of heaven. This is the only way for all mankind. You may have been to other countries and seen something of their wonders and beauties, but if you will not be born again you will never see Immanuel's land, that land that is fairer than day. You may have wandered through great forests and seen some of the monarchs of the forest as they raise their kingly heads high into the air, but if you are not born again you will never see the tree of life whose leaves are for the healing of the nations. You may have floated down some of the great rivers of the world and been amazed at their greatness, but unless you are born again you will never see the river of life that flows from the Throne of God and the Lamb. You may have dwelt in the mansions of the wealthy and mighty, and gazed on their grandeur and splendour, but if you are not born again you will never see the mansion that is prepared for those who love Him. You may have seen the rulers and kings of the world and envied their position and pomp and power, but if you are not born again you will never see the King in His glory - the King of kings and Lord of lords. You may have seen their crowns and coronets, representing fabulous wealth, but if you are not born again you will never see the crown of Glory that the Lord has for those who love His appearing. You may have sung the songs of the world and been ravished with their music, and felt the charm of their music and words, or you may have heard the world's great singers and felt you were almost in heaven, but if you are not born again you will never hear the song of Moses and the Lamb, or join in the Blood passion song they sing before the Throne. You may have sat down at many a marriage feast and entered into all the joys of that festive occasion, but if you are not born again you will never sit down at the marriage feast of the Lamb in the Glory. You have closed the eyes of your loved, mother, or father, or wife, or brother, or sister. They have fallen asleep in Jesus. Unless you are born again you will never see them again. You have bidden them an eternal farewell. Mother, it isn't long since you closed the eyes of your darling baby. It hadn't been long with you, but long enough to twine the tendrils of its affection around your heart. It is gone, and life hasn't been the same since. There is a void in life, and a greater one in your heart since that wee darling was taken from your breast. What you would not give to see it again!

"Sweet little darling, light of the home,
looking for someone, beckoning come.

Bright as a sunbeam, pure as the dew,
anxiously looking, mother, for you."

Oh, mother, if you are not born again, you will never meet your darling child again, and it will be without its mother through all eternity. Ye MUST be born again if you - YOU - would enter the kingdom of heaven. What ails you at Christ? What spite have you at your own soul? Why will you damn it when God delights to save it and gave Jesus to die for it?

"There is life for a look at the Crucified One,
There is life at this moment for thee.
Then look ,sinner, look unto Him and be saved,
Unto Him who was nailed to the tree."

Look - Look - Look - And Live.

What must I do to be Saved?

❖

'*Believe*' Acts 16: 30-31

What a mystery this word 'BELIEVE' is to many, and a stumbling block to not a few. I used to think, before I understood its meaning that it was a word "coined" by the Lord to keep as many as He could from salvation. "Believe!" Why, I never did anything else but believe. I was no heathen or infidel. I had been brought up in a godly Presbyterian home to believe in the Bible and the standards of the Church. I would have been very indignant if you had told me I didn't believe. I certainly believed the Bible. I believed Jesus was God and that He died for our sins according to the Scriptures. I believed there was a hell and there was a heaven, and still I was galloping to hell as fast as time and my feet could carry me, as happy and care free as anyone could be. I would have landed there, too, if I hadn't been arrested by the Lord Jesus and washed in His precious blood. "Happy Day!" If the Lord had said I could be saved by jumping over the moon, I would know I'd never be saved, because that would be impossible; but I would have understood what He meant. If He had said, "Make a million pounds and I'll save you," I would have known what He meant, and understood why so many are selling all to amass a fortune. Or if He had said, "Do the best you can and live a good life and I'll save you," I would have understood that, but to tell me to "BELIEVE" when I never did anything else all my life but "believe," seemed as if He was trying to mystify and perplex me.

ITS IMPORTANCE

Let us remember the importance of rightly believing, for our eternal destiny will be determined by it. We are saved by believing in Christ as our Saviour, Lord and Master, and we are all damned by our disbelieving. "Whosoever believeth in Him should not perish but have everlasting life." "He that believeth NOT the Son shall not see life, but the wrath of God ABIDETH (keeps on abiding) on him." There are only two classes - believers and UN-believers. We are saved by believing, not by works - good or bad - or by Church, sacraments, or ceremonies, but by believing in Christ. We are damned by DIS-believing in Christ. That is the only sin that damns a soul. We are not damned because we were born in sin, or because Adam fell, or because we are cursing, swearing, drunken men or women. Oh, no! The good as well as the bad are damned. Hell is packed with good people. There are no good people in heaven. Only filthy, half-damned sinners, saved by sovereign grace are there. They believed in Jesus Christ as their Saviour, and they are saved and SAFE for evermore. Hallelujah! So we see how important it is to understand what it means to BELIEVE, and know for sure we are saved.

ERRONEOUS VIEWS

Let us look at some of the erroneous and popular views there are today, and it will help us, I trust, to see more clearly when we come to consider what it means to believe and be saved, and to KNOW it.

1. The Rationalistic View.

That is, the mere assent of the mind to revealed truth. For instance, someone asks you, "Do you believe John 3: 16?" or they tell you to put your name in there instead of "whosoever". Because you believe this, then you are saved. Oh, no. There is not a devil or a damned soul does not believe John 3: 16, but that doesn't mean they are saved. I believe it is right here where the weakness of our evangelistic work lies. Anxious souls are led into the enquiry rooms and are shown John 3: 16, or some familiar passage, and are asked if they believe it. If they do, they are told they are saved. Fellow-workers, we are only making them twice over the children of hell! I remember holding a mission in a city in the USA. After the meeting, a young Presbyterian minister came to me and asked me if he might walk home with me as he would like a chat about spiritual things. As we walked along he said, "Mr. N., all I have is a few words on a piece of paper, I cannot say I KNOW I am saved. I believe all right, but I'm not sure I'm saved." He told me that as a young man 15 years before this he had gone to an evangelistic campaign and felt convicted of sin. He had gone into the enquiry room and was dealt with by one of the personal workers. He was shown John 3: 16 and asked did he believe it. He said he did. Then he was told he was saved, and he signed a card. He had joined church afterwards and by and by gone on for the ministry. There are many like this in our churches today, and they wonder how anyone can say they KNOW they are saved. It often annoys and irritates them to hear those who know they are saved testifying about it. They may even deny its possibility, and say they are sinning presumptuously in their testimony. We know we can never be saved apart from the Word of God, but we are not saved by merely believing it. We are saved by believing in Jesus Christ as our personal Saviour, and we are SURE we are saved by believing the Word of God. For instance, if you ask me, "Are you married?" I answer, "Yes." You say, "How do you know?" I produce my marriage certificate and show you that. Is that all I have to prove and assure me I am married? If that is all, that would be a queer sort of married life. I have something more than a mere "piece of paper" to assure me I am married. I HAVE MY WIFE! I have something more than a piece of paper to assure me I am saved. I have the Lord Jesus Christ living and abiding within. How many there are in our churches who have gone through the Communicant's Class and would have answered all the questions satisfactorily. They have assented to all the truth they were taught and were told they are now "Believers" therefore ready to become church members. If this is all they have, they are still children of wrath even as others and on the road to hell, and surer of getting there than they ever were before. They are wrapped around with their self-righteous rags and lulled to sleep in a carnal security, and it will be a mighty miracle if they are ever awakened and saved.

2. The Roman Catholic View.

That is, that faith or believing has some intrinsic value. The more faith you have the more you will receive. That is, believing is some sort of good work and therefore will merit favour and blessing from God. If this is true then hell is an impossibility for there are no unbelieving souls there. They all believe. The very devils believe and tremble. The only place you can find unbelievers is on earth. There are none in heaven and none in hell. Belief in itself is nothing, it is the object of our belief that determines its nature and character. If we believe in ourselves and our so-called good works, or in our church connection and church going or sacraments or ordinances, we'll be damned. But if we believe in Jesus Christ as our personal Saviour, we'll be saved and kept safe. If our faith is as a grain of mustard seed, said Jesus, we'll remove mountains. It isn't the size of our faith, but the vitality and object that counts. If our faith, however small or weak, is a living faith in God, we'll be sure we are saved and rejoice in our salvation.

3. Then there is the Fatalistic View.

That is, that if God does not give you the power to believe you will never believe. That is true, but you forget that God has given you the power to believe. When God made you He made you with the capacity to believe in Him. Just as He gave eyes to see with, ears to hear with, and a mind to think with, so He has given you the ability to believe in Him. God never made an infidel. **An infidel is a human monstrosity.** It takes a lot of time thinking before a man can make himself an infidel. It is natural to believe in God. It is unnatural to doubt. A child has no difficulty in believing. That is why so many are converted when they are children. It would be just as ridiculous for me to say, "I cannot see unless God gives me eyes" (Well, God has given you eyes, use them and you'll see) as to say, "I cannot believe unless God gives me faith" (Well, God has given you faith, use it). We couldn't live in this world if we couldn't and didn't believe. We are believing all the time. We believe as we read our news-paper. We believe in the milkman when we take our jug out for the milk. How do you know whether he'll give you the milk, and not chalk and water? You believe in him. You work all week for your employer and believe he will give you your wages, and he does. It is just the same sort of belief that brings salvation and blessing. Take God at His word and He will never fail you. To sit still and wait for something to happen to enable you to believe is to damn your soul and dishonour God. What a monster God would be if He did not make us capable of believing, and yet damned us for not doing so. What cruelty it would be on God's part if he gave His Son to die for our sins and thus provide for us a Saviour, and yet make us incapable of believing in Him and being saved.

AN ILLUSTRATION

I remember I was on a sailing vessel many years ago, bound for Valparaiso. After we had rounded Cape Horn, our cargo shifted and the vessel almost capsized. We cut away all masts to ease her, but she was on her beam end. We sat huddled together on the weather side, expecting every lurch to land us in a watery grave. The wind was shrieking like fury. The sea was like miniature mountains. Next day a large sailing vessel hove in sight. Seeing our calamity she came as near as she could and hove too, lowered a boat and pulled towards us. She couldn't come very near, there was so much wreckage around and the sea was running mountains high, so they called out for us to jump overboard and they would pick us up. We looked at each other in dismay, for we had been 48 hours or more without food and we were almost frozen stiff with cold. To jump overboard would have been suicide. When they saw we were not making any attempt, they made their way back to the vessel and were hauled on board. She trimmed her sails and made away on her course and left us to our fate. Do you mean to say that God would play a trick like that on us? Bring salvation near to us and know - because He made us so - we couldn't accept it, then leave us to our doom? There are those who believe in a LIMITED atonement who say this very thing. They say Jesus died for only a limited number. Yet God says, "Whosoever" will may come - but He is only fooling those who are not amongst the number or elect. Such an attitude and belief is making God out dishonest and a brutal monster. God is sincere when He offers salvation to "WHOSOEVER" will, for Jesus Christ - the Lamb of God - who took away the sins of the whole world, made it possible for all to be saved. "He is the propitiation for our sins and not for ours only, but for the sins of the WHOLE WORLD." Whether we can ever reconcile God's sovereignty and man's free will or not, one thing we may be sure of, none are lost because they COULD NOT believe, but because they WOULD NOT. "Ye will not come unto Me," said Jesus. I believe the old coloured preacher explained it well when preaching on election. He said if a man wants to be elected to some Government office, he must stand for election and if he gains the majority vote he is elected. So it is with the sinner. If he is to be elected to eternal life he must stand for election, and if he does he is most surely elected. What ridiculous folly on our part to sit still and say, "If I am elected I'll be elected, and if not I'll not." Such a fatalistic attitude as that is dishonouring to God and damning to the soul. Fatalism is eternally fatal for the soul. Believe at once and be saved. You are able to do it, and will be held responsible for not doing it.

PERSONAL WORKERS

As personal workers we need to be very careful when dealing with an anxious soul. To merely say, "Believe", and not explain it, we may do eternal harm to a soul. Everyone has not the same experience. We are all different in our personality and therefore our experience of believing will be different. You remember Saul of Tarsus was led to believe through the WILL. "What wilt thou have me to do?" The eunuch was led to believe through the INTELLECT. "Understandest thou what thou readest?" Philip asked him. The jailor was led to believe through the CONSCIENCE and in terror he cried out, "What must I do to be saved?" Lydia's heart was opened and she was led to believe through her EMOTIONS. So you see no two are led to believe along the same lines, but all must believe in Jesus Christ as their personal Saviour if they are to be saved. Don't let us try and make everyone believe as we did. Let us make sure we lead everyone we deal with to Christ. Some only believe after a dreadful harrowing experience, and they think everyone must have the same experience as they had. You remember our Lord opened the eyes of the blind man in John 9 by spitting on the clay and anointing his eyes with it and sending him to a pool to wash, which he did and received his sight. But when the Lord opened the eyes of Bartimaeus He merely said, "Receive thy sight," and suddenly his eyes were opened and he received his sight. Could you imagine these two men meeting in Jerusalem one day and having a hot argument about how they received their sight. The man born blind in John 9 would say, "You did not get your sight in the right way. I had to have my eyes anointed and walk miles and dip in a pool, and you say you received yours suddenly and not even anointed or walked a foot. You didn't get your sight right." Or if Bartimaeus said to John 9, "You are all wrong, you haven't received your sight in the right way. Feelings and long anxiety are not necessary." etc. Now what would we think of these two men if they behaved like that? We would consider they were crazy, and yet how many Christians act just in that way when it comes to believing in Christ for salvation. Some think one cannot really believe unless they are in an agony for weeks and go through some religious ceremony or other, such as an after-meeting, or go into an enquiry room, or by being baptised. Friend, never bother about HOW you believed, but be sure WHO you believed in for salvation. Your experience will always be unique. You will have a story to tell of "the love that sought you and the blood that bought you" that no one has ever told or ever will tell.

Saved and Sure

---　❖　---

"Believe on the Lord Jesus Christ and thou shalt be saved, and thy house."
Acts 16: 31 *"Therefore it is of faith, that it might be by grace; to the end
the promise might be sure to all."* Romans 4: 16

This old earth has had many an earthquake, but never one just like this one at Philippi, that was the strange means of leading the jailor and his family to Christ. The earthquake came suddenly and at midnight. There is nothing unusual in this, for this is how they usually start. But here is the unusual: The foundations of the prison were shaken. All the prison doors were opened, and everyone's bonds were loosed. Yet not a prisoner escaped or even attempted to escape. The thing was so unusual that the jailor drew out his sword and would have killed himself, supposing that the prisoners had fled. Paul cried out in a loud voice, "Do thyself no harm, for we are all here." Then he called for a light and sprang in and came trembling and fell down before Paul and Silas and brought them out and said, "Sirs, what must I do to be saved?"

It took this unusual earthquake to break the hard-hearted, cruel , Roman soldier down and compel him to cry out, "What must I do to be saved?" God has strange ways and uses strange means to bring sinners to their senses and compel them to realise they are lost sinners and need salvation. When sinners become full grown and become fascinated with the world and its pleasures and sin, they have become used to their own notions and ways, no ordinary means will bring them to a sense of their danger, so God uses the unusual. Some sudden calamity occurs, some sudden death of a loved one. Sudden sickness overtakes them; their health vanishes; their money takes wings and flies away. One strange thing after another comes like a bolt out of the blue, until their life is one succession of tragedies; until, like the jailor, they feel like ending it all by committing suicide. Just at that point they are led to feel their help- less, lost condition, and cry out, "What must I do to be saved?"

There are many everywhere who thank God for the terrible and trying experience that God used to make them conscious of their lost condition and seek to be saved.

THE HARD WAY

It is the hard way to Christ. His love and mercy and good- ness were all unavailing to lead to repentance, so to save your soul He had to do the hard and the unusual. What a **lover** He is! He will not let you go to hell without using every means, usual and unusual, hard or easy, to bring you to Himself. He will take your children; He will lay you on your back in sickness and pain; He will thwart your every move and blight your every hope; He will burn your barns and blight your crops, but He will save your soul. He **cannot compel you to be saved**, but He will use every means **to make you willing** to be saved. No lost soul can blame God for not doing all he could to save them.

SECRET SEEKERS

I believe there are many who know they are not saved and are yearning to know how to be saved and sure about it. They are timid, shy and retiring. They could never make their need known, even to their nearest and dearest friend. Yet all the time they are anxious about their soul and long to know how to be saved. They know and feel they are lost, although they live respectable, religious lives. They may be zealous church workers and members. Their very lives and outward profession make it all the harder for them to be saved; for everyone thinks they are alright. Their parents and ministers would be shocked if they were told they were unsaved. When they joined the church they were sure something would take place and they would know they were saved. But nothing happened. How deeply and strangely they were moved the first time they went to Communion. They felt, surely something will happen today. They took the bread and wine and nothing happened. Only God knows the feeling of disappointment they endured. So they have gone on through the years **professing** but not **possessing** - everyone taking it for granted they are saved. Oh, the agony of such a soul. Between the fear of being for ever lost and their pride, their live is a veritable hell of torment. If only God would save them and "save their face." They would be saved at once, but to confess that all their good works and good life were only a hollow sham - it is too sore on their pride and so they continue longing to be saved. If they only made known their need to some saved friend, they might be saved at once. They are ignorant of God's righteousness and going about to establish their own righteousness, have not submitted themselves unto the righteousness of God. I believe even preachers take too much for granted when preaching. We think all many need is to be urged to decide for Christ. We plead with them to do so now, while all the time many of them would do so if they only knew "how".

Friend! I will try the best I know how to tell you what you must do to be saved and be sure about it. Will you read carefully the following and pray the Holy Spirit will make it clear to you and enable you to do it?

FOUR THINGS

There are at least four things you must know and do if you are to be saved and sure about it.

1. You must take your place as a Sinner unsaved.

Never mind about your godly parents and your upbringing and your good life and religious ceremonies and activities. You are just a poor sinner. You may be accomplished and amiable and well educated; but you are only an accomplished child of the devil, an amiable heir of wrath, and an educated servant of the devil. You are lost and ruined; your heart is deceitful above all things and desperately wicked. You are an ungodly sinner - condemned already - the wrath of God abiding on you - judgment ahead of you and hell beneath you. You are helpless and undone. You cannot do a single thing to save your soul. All your best religious works are only filthy rags in God's sight. You are utterly unworthy and undone. You can never do anything to deserve God's salvation. You can never forget God in your debt or under obligation to save you. You are and always will be undeserving and hell-deserving. This is God's truth about you and every unsaved sinner . Will you take your place as such a sinner? These are the only ones Jesus died to save, and saves. He came not to call the righteous, but sinners - real, thorough-bred, bona-fide sinners. If you have a good word to say for yourself or a good deed to offer for an atonement for your soul, you will never be saved. You must come as you are, taking your place with sinners of every kind, for there is no difference - all have sinned. God hasn't a salvation for good sinners, church sinners, or bad sinners. Oh, no, the same salvation is only for the lost, guilty sinners, good or bad, religious or irreligious. This is sore on your pride. People will be amazed at your being saved after all the years of good living and religious activity. Never mind. Your pride will damn you, but never help to save you.

2. Yield yourself unreservedly to Christ.

Full surrender. No withholding - friends, time, earthly store. He doesn't demand a **perfect** surrender, but He does demand an **honest** surrender. All you know and don't know, without evasion or reservation. He will take nothing less and nothing else. Love so amazing, so divine, **demands** my life, my soul, my all. You hear a lot today about - Must I give up this or that? You must give up **everything**. Let the unrighteous man forsake His ways and the ungodly man his thoughts and let him turn to the Lord and He will abundantly pardon. Jesus doesn't save everybody. Oh, no, He saves **His** people. "His name shall be called Jesus for He shall save **His** people." If you are not willing to belong to Christ you can never be saved. "Now to be Thine, yea, Thine alone, O Lamb of God I come," must be the language and attitude of your heart. You must break clean, once and for all, with the world, flesh and the devil. A clean cut and a whole-hearted surrender. You cannot serve God and the devil, but you must serve one or the other **all** the time. Neither God nor the devil will take **part-time** service. They both demand whole time, whole-hearted surrender. So many would like to make Jesus a Saviour merely from hell. A sort of a fire escape out of hell-fire into heaven, but they want to live as they like and do as they please - enjoy the world and its pleasures and yet escape the world's doom and damnation. It can't be done, friend. You must make a clean break.

"Forsake all," says Jesus. Take up the cross and follow Him. Don't be frightened to yield your all. If He loved you enough to die for you, surely you won't be afraid to trust Him fully. His yoke is easy and His burden is light. His commands are not grievous. He will satisfy every longing and never leave you nor forsake you. Don't be frightened. Let go all, and for ever. You will never live to regret it.

3. Ask the Lord to save you.

Isn't it strange we find it hard to do this. We are so proud and stuck up. We dislike to be under obligation to anybody, even God. To get down on your knees and confess you are a lost, undone, guilty sinner, and tell Him you will be His and His alone, and ask Him to save you now, seems about the hardest thing anyone can ask you to do. If God would only save you without you having to pray, it would be easier for you. If He would only pander to your pride and cater to your conceit, even a wee bit, it would make it easier for you. You must ask if you are to receive; knock if the door is to be opened; seek, if you are to find. "Whosoever shall call upon the name of the Lord shall be saved." The Lord will never force you to be saved, He only comes where He is wanted and welcomed. I am not saying you must **say** prayers. Oh no, but you must **pray**. The heathen say prayers. You could train a parrot to say prayers. You are not far from the kingdom when you begin to pray and stop saying prayers.

> "I often **say** my prayers, but do I ever pray?
> Do the wishes of my heart dictate the words I say?
> I may as well kneel down and worship gods of stone
> As offer to the living God the prayer of words alone;
> For words without the heart the Lord will never hear,
> Nor will e'er that man regard whose prayers are not sincere."

4. Receive Jesus Christ by faith as your Saviour, and His death as the atonement for your sins.

"To as many as received Him to them gives He power to become the sons of God." This is the crux of the whole matter. There are many who are truly conscious of their lost, undone condition before God and gladly and fully yield themselves to Christ and pray and pray sincerely for the Lord to save them, and keep on praying and living in misery and anxiety about their soul's salvation. Why? Is God hard to persuade? Is He unwilling to save? Are they too bad to be saved? Have they committed the unpardonable sin? Oh no, the reason is they don't accept what is so freely offered them. They ask but they don't receive, because they won't or are frightened they are presuming on God. You must exercise faith by taking Him at His word, without any feeling, if necessary. It is the venture of faith. You see faith without works is dead. When you confess your lost condition and yield fully to Christ and ask Him to save you; this only **qualifies** you for salvation. You don't **merit** salvation because you do all this. Oh no, you put yourself in the place where God can and does save you, when you accept Christ as your own personal Saviour. Don't be frightened to venture on Christ.

> "Upon a life I did not live,
> Upon a death I did not die,
> Another's life, another's death,
> I stake my whole eternity."

Thou shalt never perish, but **have** everlasting life. None perish that receive Him. You can never trust yourself too little or Christ too much. It is not presumption to accept Christ as your Saviour. It's your privilege as a lost, guilty sinner. God offers Him to you freely on the ground of grace. Receive the gift.

Have you done this? Can you now say, "Thank God I am saved."

THE WITNESS OF THE SPIRIT

Have you the witness of the Spirit, witnessing to your spirit that you are saved? Remember, when you truly accept Christ as your Saviour, the Spirit answers to the Blood and tells you you are born of God. So you don't say, "I **hope** I am saved, or I **think** I am saved, or I **believe** or **trust** I am saved." You say, "**I know** I am saved." No one but yourself can tell whether you sincerely take your place as a lost sinner and yield yourself fully to Christ and sincerely ask Him to save you and really do receive Him as your personal Saviour. But while I cannot see your heart and know what goes on there, as I thus try to lead you to Christ, I can surely know whether, "'Tis done, the great transaction's done" by this fact: you will be able to feel and say, "I see it." "Now **I know** I am saved." If you can't say this, it's because you are not truly sincere. You see you can't fool God. You can fool yourself or me, but you can't deceive God. Just as certainly as two and two make four, fire burns, so certainly when you truly take your place as a guilty, lost sinner, and yield fully to Christ and ask Him to save you, and receive Him by faith as your own personal Saviour, you **know** you are saved. Don't fool yourself or let others try to. God never lies. He gives you the assurance of your salvation.

SOMETHING WRONG

If you haven't this assurance, there is something wrong. Let me help you about this. You are not sure because you are **doubting** His word. He plainly says, "Whosoever believeth **hath** everlasting life.," "Him that cometh to me I will in no wise cast out." Could anything be plainer? Surely if you trust a person you will show it by believing what he says. Just imagine you saying, I trust you but I don't believe your word. He that believeth not the word maketh God a **liar**. You say, "I do believe His word and yet I can't say, 'I **know** I am saved'." Then it is because you **disobey**. There is something you are quibbling with God about. Some restitution you know you should make. Someone you should apologise to and ask their forgiveness. Some debt you should pay, **maybe** long forgotten. It may be the Lord wants you to make a public confession of your salvation, without any feeling on your part, say you are saved. The feeling will come alright when you obey. You see the Spirit - the witness - is given to those who **believe** and to those who **obey**. If you believe and don't obey you will never be sure. If you obey and don't believe you will never be sure. **Trust** and **obey** for there is **no other way**. When you truly believe and obey the Spirit immediately and consciously seals you and assures you that you are saved. Then you have peace with God. You heart will sing, "I **know** He is mine. Ten thousand charms around Him shine, but best of all I **know** He is mine." This is a real Bible, heart, **know-so** salvation. Be satisfied with nothing else and nothing less.

Save Yourselves

❖

"Save yourselves from this untoward generation" Acts 2: 40

These were the closing words of Peter's pentecostal sermon: the first sermon preached in the Christian Church. What a sermon it was! And what a preacher!

We hardly recognise him. What a change has been wrought in him since Christ died! Before Pentecost what a blustering, blundering coward he was. He could swear and curse better than he could preach. But now see him stand before these murderers of Christ and hear his bold and scriptural words, so eloquently and heroically spoken. No cowardice here; no cursing and swearing now. Goodbye to all that forever. And what marvellous results! Think of it. In Jerusalem of all places: the seat and citadel of all bigotry and hatred of Christ. And Jews of all people. The very ones who had cried out only a few days prior to this: "Crucify Him! Crucify Him!" Now they are crying out from pricked hearts, "Men and brethren, what shall we do?" Just imagine! 3000 of them. What a scene! What an event! (O Lord, send us another Pentecost these last of the last days. Surely our hungry hearts cry out for it?) When Peter heard their cry, he immediately stopped his preaching and told them how to be saved - what to do; and with many other words did he testify and exhort, saying, "Save yourselves from this untoward generation."

STARTLING STATEMENT

These were strange and startling words to use in instructing new converts. They are startling and strange to many today too, when we hear so many told, "Once saved, always saved." "You are as sure of heaven as if you were already there." They seem to infer to the convert that all has been done and they needn't have another care or concern. You can sin and live in sin, but it's all right, you are saved. You can backslide, and live a backsliden life and go to heaven. One of these chaps told me he could murder, rob or commit adultery, lie and cheat, curse and swear, and still be saved. "You see," he said, "when I decided for Christ He saved me." I told him that sounded queer to me, for he had unborn himself when he decided for Christ. By birth he was a child of the devil, and when he decided for Christ he was unborn or born **again**. If he did it once, could he not do it again? I am not discussing could one be saved and lost. What I am trying to do is to urge all believers to "save themselves" because they are saved. The feeling some give you is that salvation is something like taking out an insurance policy. You secure the policy and pay your premiums. You are covered, no matter how, or where, you live. Just as long as you pay your premiums you are all right. Your character and manner of life have not been changed. You are the same chap; live the same worldly way, but you are insured - you are saved. This is the impression these "Once saved, always saved" professors give you. As long as you profess you are saved, you can live as you have always lived; your character isn't changed, nor your conduct. You can love the world and its pleasures, as you have always done and still you are "covered" - you are saved. Such teaching is soul-damning and destructive of that old, and old-fashioned doctrine of "Work out your own salvation" and "Save yourselves from this untoward generation." It destroys all incentive to "Follow peace with all men, **and holiness**, without which no man shall see the Lord, looking diligently lest any man shall fail of the grace of God." It ignores the solemn admonitions "that we be not slothful, but followers of them who through faith and patience (persistent perseverance) inherit the promises." "Cast not away therefore your confidence, which hath great recompense of reward for ye have need of patience (persistent perseverance) after that ye have done the will of God, ye might receive the promise." Dear friends, salvation is no lazy and easy road to heaven, as many seem to think. It's a race, and we are to run with dogged determination the race set before us, looking unto Jesus. Paul could say, "I therefore **so** run, not so uncertainly (carelessly, lazily): so fight I, not as one that beateth the air; but I keep under my body and bring it into subjection, lest by any means, when I have preached to others I myself should be a "castaway". This word is used only 8 times in the original New Testament. (Once 'castaway' I Cor. 9:27; once 'rejected' Heb. 6: 8; and six times 'reprobate' 2 Cor. 13: 5,6,7, 2 Tim. 3: 8 and Tit. 1: 16). It would seem as if Paul was urged to "run" and "fight" and keep at it, or he might lose more than the reward. He feels he might lose the race by being disqualified.

TWO SIDES TO SALVATION

There are two sides to salvation - God's side and man's side. The Divine and the human. God can't do my part; I can't do God's part. God can't repent for me. God can't accept Christ for me. I can't save myself. I can't forgive my sins. I can't regenerate myself. But when I do my part - repent, believe, accept Christ; God saves me, pardons my sins and regenerates me. There is just as much common sense about the preservation of my physical life as there is about the preservation of my spiritual life. God can't breathe the air for me; God can't exercise for me; God can't eat food for me; God can't drink water for me. I can't give myself life - that is God's work. But if I do my part in taking care of life, eating regularly and sufficiently, breathing fresh air and taking exercise, God will and does bless these means used by me to give me a healthy and strong life. Wouldn't it be ridiculous and nonsensical of me to expect a healthy, happy life and be careless about eating, drinking, breathing and exercising. How long would I live under such circumstances? Yet there are many who believe all this about our physical life and either ignore it or deny it, for their spiritual life. "Oh," they say, "I am saved, and that's all there is to it," and they never seem to hear the Lord say, "Save yourselves from this untoward generation." If I never use the means of grace provided for my spiritual life, how long will my spiritual life last? What sort of a spiritual life will it be before it expires? So we see it is hard work and constant and costly work if we are to "save ourselves from this untoward generation."

"UNTOWARD GENERATION"

Notice it is an 'untoward generation'. Because we are saved, that doesn't mean the devil is dead or this "vile world is a friend of grace", and we'll never be tempted or tested. Oh, no! It is the same old world and devil, and until we leave it for our "inheritance incorruptible and undefiled and that never fades away" it will be an enemy of ours. It is, and always will be, a 'perverse', 'crooked', generation. Jesus has revealed to us the sort of world it is. "An evil and adulterous generation." "A wicked generation."

"Faithless and perverse". "Sinful and adulterous." "A generation of vipers." These are strong and graphic statements and are given to warn us and urge us to "save ourselves from it." Peter not only tells them to do it, but also **how** to do it.

HOW TO SAVE OURSELVES

Let us consider for a while his instructions, and may we not only consider them, but lay them to heart and carry them out in our daily lives. We will have to if we are to "save ourselves" from this "untoward generation."

1. Be baptised (v 38). This is our privilege and duty and necessary to our continuance in **the** way. It will be an open and symbolic confession of our turning from sin and the world and accepting Christ as our personal Saviour. We are buried with Christ and now risen to newness of life, to walk with Christ **in** the world, but not **of** the world. Don't begin to quibble about the **mode** of the sacrament; it is the **fact** that counts. We are not told how much water we are to come under - whether a few drops or gallons. Be sure of one thing - "be baptised," and suit yourself about the mode. Have a **quiet** conscience about it, or Satan will fret and worry you over it. Be persuaded **in your own mind** and don't let others be a conscience for you or you'll never be satisfied.

There are two baptisms mentioned: There is **John's** baptism which is water. "John truly baptised with water." Acts 1:5. "I indeed baptise you with water unto repentance." Matt. 3: 11. Then there is **Jesus'** baptism which is "with the Holy Ghost." Acts 1: 5. "But ye shall be baptised with the Holy Ghost." Matt. 3: 11. "He (Jesus) shall baptised you with he Holy Ghost and fire." Jesus taught the disciples about the baptism with the Holy Ghost. Acts 11: 16. "Then remembered I the word of the Lord, how **He** said ("used to be saying" - margin) John indeed baptised with water, but ye shall be baptised with the Holy Ghost." There are so many true believers today who firmly believe and adhere to water baptism, but altogether omit the baptism with the Holy Ghost, or deny its necessity, if we are to "save ourselves". The converts of the early Church were sometimes baptised with water **before** they were baptised with the Holy Ghost. Sometimes they were baptised with water **after** they were baptised **with the Holy Ghost**. But whether before or after, they were Spirit baptised believers. This Spirit-baptism is not 'conversion' or 'regeneration'. It is one thing to be baptised **into the body** and quite another to be baptised **with the Holy Ghost.** The first baptism is the work of the Spirit the second is the work of Jesus Christ. The first you receive when you repent and believe in Jesus; the second you receive when you surrender fully and receive by faith the blessing.

The one is as **necessary** as the other and just as **real**. If we are to be saved we must be **"born again"** or baptised into the body. If we are to "save ourselves" we must be baptised with the Holy Ghost and fire. Don't try and "save yourselves from this untoward generation," for it is not by might or power but by the Spirit we are enabled to "save ourselves". The Spirit-baptism is always subsequent to conversion. **After** you are saved you must be baptised with the Holy Ghost if you are to succeed in "saving yourself." Become a candidate at once for this baptism. Jesus alone is the Baptiser - and you will be enabled to save yourself.

2. 'They continued' (v. 42). This is the only way anyone will continue. It is a long drawn-out, ever present, work. It will never be finished until we are 'saved to sin no more.' It is a hard, uphill, every day, every hour business. You cannot continue alone. You will grow weary and faint in your mind if you try to do it alone. It is only as the Spirit is depended on entirely and constantly that we will make progress. It's too big a task for any man - any saved man - to tackle without the Spirit. How did they continue? - **steadfastly**. These were no up and down, off and on converts. And **daily**. Every day, everywhere, they continued. Good days, bad days, hard days, easy days, joyful days, sad days, sick days, well days, home days, holidays, warm days, cold days - **daily**.

What did they daily and steadfastly continue in?

(i) **Doctrine.** They were Bible-believers. They daily took time to read and study their Bible. They were not carried about with every wind of doctrine.

(ii) **Fellowship.** They joined Church. They lived at peace with their fellow believers. They were not quarrelsome. They were unoffending and unoffended. Bitterness and malice, envy and jealousy, questioning and quarrelling, were alien to them.

(iii) **Breaking Bread.** Not only in the Church but in their homes. Every meal was a sacrament. They ate with gladness and singleness of heart. What a blessed time their Communion services were. No quarrelling or bickering; and what happy homes they had. They were filled with gladness and singleness of heart.

(iv) **And in Prayers.** They took time and trouble to pray - and it takes both. The prayer meeting found them present and the family altar was erected in every home and family prayers were offered. Private prayers were not neglected. Notice it was 'prayers', not 'prayer' - all sorts of prayers and they daily and steadfastly continued at it.

3, **Praising God** (v 47). Praising is just as essential as praying. The one has to be acquired and cultivated as much as the other. They go well together, if we are to succeed in "saving ourselves from this untoward generation."

The children of Israel were made captive because they served **not** the Lord their God with **joyfulness** and with **gladness** of heart. A growling, grumbling, morbid and morose disposition neither pleases God nor helps us to save ourselves, so let us see to it that we allow nothing to destroy our joy in the Lord and the continued song of praise in our lives. We are to be careful for nothing, prayerful about everything and thankful for anything.

This is the sort of life that brings blessing to others in the church and in the world. "**And** the Lord added to the Church daily such as should be saved." v 47. The saving of souls follows as naturally as 'cause and effect' when we continue 'saving ourselves from this untoward generation.' It is only as we are saved and being saved that we are the means of saving others. Laziness and holiness are mutually antagonistic. The Christian life is no 'flowery bed of ease.' It will mean hard and constant work if we are to endure to the end. The Lord has made full provision for our every daily need, so as to ensure continued and final success in 'saving ourselves from this untoward generation.'

> *Are there no foes for me to face?*
> *Must I not stem the flood?*
> *Is this vile world a friend to grace*
> *To help me on to God?*

> *Since I must fight if I would reign,*
> *Increase my courage, Lord,*
> *I'll bear the toil, endure the pain,*
> *Supported by Thy Word.*

Cross-Bearing

---❖---

'And whosoever doth not bear His cross and come after Me cannot be My disciple' Luke 14: 27

C ross bearing was the law of discipleship when Christ was here on earth in the days of His flesh and **is** the law today everywhere and for everybody. Notice the word 'whosoever'. It means everyone who would be His disciple today. It includes every disciple or would-be disciple and excludes none. Christ's condition or law of discipleship isn't changed to suit every candidate for discipleship. He will never change the law to secure a disciple. It is for all ages. There are those who would have us distinguish between being a 'Christian' and a 'Disciple'. Jesus knew no such distinction. Notice His words: "There went great multitudes with Him and He turned and said unto **them**, not merely disciples, but the **multitudes**." v 25. Then in v 26 He said: "If any man" not merely disciple - ANY MAN. Also Mark 8: 34, "And when He had called the people unto Him, **with His disciples.**" Here we have the people and the disciples separately mentioned, showing the law of discipleship was not merely for the disciples alone but for everyone who would be a disciple of the Lord Jesus. How conspicuous and emphatic and repeated this law of discipleship was in the teachings of Jesus. Isn't it very significant and ominous, the silence in our teaching and preaching today. We seem more concerned about making Christ and salvation popular and appealing than we are about the law of discipleship. Our concern in His service seems to be success and large tabulated results. Someone has said: "If we can preach the Gospel, and please the religious, natural, unregenerate man, we are not preaching Christ's Gospel." How true it is. Cross-bearing is never popular or pleasing even amongst true disciples, let alone the natural, unregenerate man. We forget we are the **salt** of the earth, not the **sugar**.

'INSISTENCY OF JESUS'

How insistent our Lord was about this law of discipleship - "Cross bearing." "If any man will come after me, let him deny himself, and **take up his cross** and follow me." Matt. 16: 24. "Whosoever will come after me, let him deny himself and **take up his cross** and follow me." Mark 8: 34. "If any man will come after me, let him deny himself and **take up his cross daily** and follow me." Luke 9: 23. Then the words of our text, "And whosoever doth not bear his cross and come after Me, CANNOT BE MY DISCIPLE."

We can be very earnest and sincere professed followers of Jesus Christ, or good, devout and diligent church members and earnest church workers, but we "cannot be His disciples". There is no avoiding or escaping the issue. If we are truly His disciples we are **daily** bearing the cross. If we are not bearing the cross, we may be what we like, but we are not His disciples.

TOO HARSH, TOO SEVERE

Spurious Christians are unwilling to believe this. They look upon such a law of discipleship as "morbid", "gloomy", "morose", "narrow-minded" - to harsh and exacting. They say we will never win men for Christ by such high and exacting demands. We must attract them by other means. Make the way of life easy and acceptable, and we may win 'converts' and church members, but we are not making disciples. We are making make-believe, spurious Christians. I believe that by lowering the standard we have made salvation cheap. It is 'free' but not 'cheap'. When you hear one who desires to become a Christian asking, "Must I give up dancing?" "Must I give up picture shows?" "Must I give up tobacco?" etc., etc., surely their conception of being His disciple is a 'cheap' thing. Imagine putting Jesus Christ and His royal service in the same scale with tobacco or a dance or show! We surely have made salvation cheap when the supposed anxious one talks like that. It isn't a question of giving up this or that. It is a question of denying self and taking up the cross - fosaking all and following Christ.

Love so amazing, so divine
Demands *my* **life**, *my* **soul**, *my* ALL.

And He will take nothing less.

"WHAT IS THE CROSS?"

There is such a lot of sentimental nonsense preached and taught about cross-bearing today. Many of our hymns and much of our poetry is filled with the same soft rubbish. You hear some saying they have a heavy cross to bear, because of some physical infirmity or malady, or because of some circumstances of life, in the home or in business or in the church. We may call this cross-bearing and give ourselves the impression that we are His disciples. Mind you, these things may result from bearing the cross Jesus mentions - but they are not 'the cross'. It is very significant to notice that you never read in the Bible about 'crosses'. It is always 'cross'. There is only one cross for every disciple, and that is His cross - CHRIST'S CROSS. What is meant by HIS cross? It is not the wooden cross. That was only the symbol of what the cross represented. The cross was the symbol of the hostile hatred of the world - the malignant, malicious, cruel treatment of mankind to Jesus Christ. They couldn't do anything more shameful or cruel to Him. There was no more cruel and shameful form of death. The lowest and most violent criminals were thus executed. In their hatred and rage at Christ they put Him to death on the cross.

PETER REBUKED

You remember how indignant Peter was when Jesus told them the cruel way He was to be put to death. "Be it far from Thee, Lord: this shall not be unto Thee." Jesus turned and rebuked him and then said, not only is the cross for Me, but for every disciple. "If any man will come after me let him deny himself and take up his cross and follow Me." Isn't it just here so many would-be disciples part company with Jesus. The cross fills them with fear and dread. The young Ruler was very anxious to gain eternal life, but when he heard the plain, uncompromising conditions: "Sell all ... take up the cross and follow Me," he went away very sorrowful. It is the same everywhere today. They want the blessing of salvation without the reproach of the cross of Christ. It can't be done, dear reader. No cross, no crown, is as true today as when Jesus said, "Ye cannot be My disciple unless you take up the cross." We must make Moses' decision ours if we are to be Christ's disciples. "By faith Moses ... choosing rather to suffer affliction with the people of God, than enjoy the pleasures of sin for a season: esteeming the **reproach of Christ** greater riches than the treasures of Egypt." It is this reproach of Christ - His cross - that is so unpopular everywhere these last of the last days. If only we could be popular with the world not ostracised by it - by becoming a disciple, multitudes would decide, but the consequences of identification with Christ either frightens them or fills them with dismay and disgust.

To the law of discipleship - cross-bearing - Jesus annexed three reasons, designed to make the obeying of it easier. (See Luke 9: 24-26). Each reason is introduced by the word "For".

THREE REASONS

1. Natural Life vs Eternal Life

"For whosoever will save his life shall lose it; but whosoever will lose his life for My sake, the same shall save it." In this startling paradox the word 'life' is used in a double sense. In the first instance in each clause of the sentence, it signifies natural life, with all the adjuncts that make it pleasant and enjoyable; in the second, it means the spiritual life of a renewed soul. The deep, pregnant saying of Jesus may therefore be thus expounded and paraphrased: Whosoever **will** save (ie. make it his business to save or preserve) his natural life and worldly well-being, shall lose the higher life, the life indeed; and whosoever is willing to lose his natural life for My sake shall find the true eternal life. According to this maxim we must lose something. It is not possible to live without sacrifice of some kind, the only question being what shall be sacrificed - the lower or the higher life: animal happiness or spiritual blessedness? If we choose the higher, we must be prepared to deny ourselves and take up the cross, though the actual amount of the loss we are called on to bear may be small: for godliness is profitable unto all things, having the promise of the life that now is as well as that which is to come.

If, on the other hand, we choose the lower and resolve to have it at all hazards, we must inevitably lose the higher. There is no escape. The soul's life and all the imperishable goods of the soul - righteousness, godliness, faith, love, patience, meekness - are the price we pay for worldly enjoyment. You say the price is too great. That is what Jesus next told His hearers as the second persuasive to cross-bearing.

2. Present Gain vs Eternal Loss

"For what is a man profited (or advantaged) if he shall gain the whole world and lose himself, or be castaway?" (Luke 9: 25). You say the sacrifice is too great. To take up the reproach of Christ - the cross - and deny self is too exacting. This is only one side of the ledger: look at and consider the other side. The fleeting, unsatisfying pleasures of life never bring contentment and don't last. They pass away like the morning clouds and early dew, but they leave an inflamed and unsatisfied desire behind, like an unquenchable fire. On the other hand, by bearing His reproach and shame - His cross - we find real joy and entire satisfaction - and it is lasting. "For what is a man advantaged if he gain the whole world and **lose himself**, or be castaway?" It is a simple question of profit and loss. It is the work of the devil to keep us looking at only one side of the question, thereby deceiving and destroying us. We are not now thinking about eternal loss or eternal gain, but present loss and present gain. You have never heard or seen or read of any true disciple repenting or being sorry for denying self and taking up the cross and following Christ. No! He glories in the cross and sings, "Jesus keep me near the cross; keep its scenes before me." But there are many who have gone in for self and self-indulgence and fleeting pleasures, and didn't find satisfaction in them, but lost themselves and became castaway. I entreat you, reader, be sure and look at both sides of the ledger ere you decide. The cross may seem rough and harsh and the self-denying hard and unnecessary, but our light affliction which is but **for a moment**, worketh for us a far more exceeding and eternal weight of glory. Hallelujah!

3   Present Shame vs Future Glory

The third argument in favour of cross-bearing is drawn from the argument to come. "For whosoever shall be ashamed of Me and My words, of him shall the Son of Man be ashamed when He shall come in His own glory and in his Father's and of the holy angels." And as Matthew continues (Matt. 16: 27): "And He shall reward every man according to his works." This is the future side of the bargain, and it is well we should consider cross-bearing in the light of it. Cross-bearing is not only good and satisfying in this life; in the life to come it will bring sure and great reward. O may we live with eternity's values in view. What fools we are if we shrink from and refuse the cross and choose this world's pleasures and gains. We will be disappointed and dissatisfied in this life and rejected at the judgment. Five minutes after you are dead, how will these things appear?

The hope set before the disciple here is one which maketh not ashamed. It will most surely be realised. As certainly as the true disciples have to suffer now, so certainly will there come a time when they shall be rewarded with eternal glory. It is a righteous thing (not merely a benevolent thing) in God to grant a recompense of rest and joy in the world to come unto those who have denied self and taken up the cross for His sake in this present evil world. Hallelujah! His disciples do not suffer by **chance** but by **law**.

CERTAINTY OF REWARD

The law for all disciples is, "Bear the cross here and you shall wear the crown hereafter." From experience we know that the one part of this law does not fail, for the cross does come to every true disciple and from the unfailing certainty with which the law operates in that part which comes under our observation, we may predict the eternity of that which we see not - the future recompense promised to the true disciple.

The hope of eternal reward is not only reliable, it is a worthy motive to a self-sacrificing life. There are those who say we should do what is right, without either hope of reward or fear of punishment. Such men, it is suspected, preach a heroism they do not practice. Men who do not merely imagine, but act, have always an eternal hope in view. Christ, the greatest and purest of all heroes, cherished such a hope. "Who for the joy that was set before Him endured the cross, despising the shame, and is set down at the right hand of the Throne of God." Disciples need not be frightened of degenerating into moral vulgarity by imitating their Lord in this respect. There is no vulgarity in the virtue which is sustained by the hope of reward. That hope is not selfishness. It is simply believing in the **reality** of the kingdom for which we suffer and labour, involving, of course, the reality of each disciple's interest in it, your own not excepted. Such faith is necessary to heroism, for who would fight and suffer for a dream? It is necessary for the disciple to believe in the judgment and rewards. Where such faith and hope are not, little or no Christian heroism will be found. One of the early fathers said: "There is no certain work where there is an uncertain reward." We cannot be heroes in doubt or despair. We cannot struggle after a Divine kingdom and be sceptical whether these things be more than devout imaginations and unrealisable ideals. In such a mood we will take things easy and make secular happiness our chief concern. Thank God for the sure reward for every true cross-bearing disciple. No cross, no crown, is as true today as ever and just as sure as we bear the cross, we will wear the crown.

Surely these reasons or arguments Jesus gave His disciples, and gives us today, should encourage us to take up the cross daily and follow Him. We are His companions in tribulation. This inspiring thought turns pain into pleasure and shame into glory for every true disciple. When the Master has suffered, surely it is unseemly in the disciple to shrink from it, or complain. If we are ashamed of the cross - the reproach - He will be ashamed of us.

> "O cross, that liftest up my head,
> I dare not ask to fly from thee:
> I lay in dust life's glory dead,
> And from the ground there blossoms red,
> Life that shall endless be."

The Unpardonable Sin

❖

"Therefore, I say unto you, all manner of sin and blasphemy shall be forgiven unto men, but the blasphemy against the Holy Ghost shall not be forgiven unto men, and whosoever speaketh against the Son of Man, it shall be forgiven him; but whoever speaketh against the Holy Ghost, it shall not be forgiven him, neither in this world, neither in the world to come." Matthew 12: 31-32

I have been preaching to you, night after night, the 'forgiveness of sin.' I have endeavoured to show you God's willingness to forgive and save, and as I have made my way home after the service I have wondered what the angels thought of my message and the manner of delivering it. How cold and careless when compared to the greatness of His love, and the glory of the message of full and free forgiveness. Then I wondered what they thought of the reception given to the message by the hearers. Some believed, but the many treated it lightly, or deliberately refused it, although needing forgiveness so sorely. What a wonder it must be to the angels.

I am not preaching tonight the 'forgiveness of sin' but the 'Sin that has no forgiveness in this world or the world to come.'

MUCH CONFUSION

It is strange the amount of confusion there is concerning this sin. Some say and think that it could only have been committed when our Lord was here on earth in the days of His flesh. We know it was committed then. You remember our Lord said to the Pharisees: "You would not come." That is past tense. Towards the middle of His earthly ministry He said to the same people: "Ye will not come to Me." This is present tense, and is the reason why not every unsaved man is unsaved. You may blame everybody and everything, but it is only your will that keeps you from coming to Christ. There is not a devil in hell or a man or a circumstance on earth that can keep you from Christ, if you will to come. Then, towards the end of His ministry, He told them, "Ye cannot come; ye shall die in your sins."

COMMON TODAY

Others tell us that it is rarely, if ever, committed today. I question such a statement. I believe that it is as common, and may be more so, today than it was in the days of our Lord. If it was possible then, how much more today? I believe if I had angels' eyes I would get a vision, here and now, that would unfit me for preaching to you. There are those here tonight and they are as surely damned as any soul in hell. They are as sure of being there as if they were already there. In their bodies they carry a doomed and damned soul. Their day of grace has come and gone, and gone forever. If I could lift the skin on their foreheads I would see the brand of Cain and the curse of God, for on the forehead God has set indelibly a mark, unseen by man, for man is blind and in the dark. There never was a day when Satan was damning men by deluding them into thinking that they could be saved just when and where they liked. That they could live as long as they liked in sin, and then when they felt they could do nothing else they would call on God and the God they had spurned would be there to save and bless. There isn't a single word in all the Bible that gives any man unsaved any hope why he should not be in hell next moment. All the promises are Yea and Amen IN Christ; but you are out of Christ and without hope and God in this world. "Be not deceived, God is not mocked." You cannot make a convenience of God. You cannot live in sin and die in grace. How can we explain why so many are religiously going to hell, and yet they have the Bible in their hands and read to them? They mock God day by day, and yet hope a hope that God will not let them die in their sins and go to hell. What delusion this is! God commands every man to repent, and it is at the risk of your soul that you refuse. A man said to me one time, "What about the dying thief?" I said to him, "WHICH ONE?" There were two. One saved that none might despair. One damned that none might presume. "Which one?" Just as truly as the Lord told the Pharisees that they would die in their sins if they believed not that He was the Christ, so truly will you die in yours if you won't believe or put off believing to some more convenient time. NOW is the accepted time. NOW is the day of salvation. Tomorrow may be too late; not that you might die now, but your day of grace may end, and in that living body of yours you will carry a doomed soul. There are others who say that they have committed this sin. Their minds are filled with gloomy foreboding, and their heart with despair and darkness. They are unfit for the service of God and the society of men. Friend, let me tell you, on the authority of God's word, that you have not committed this sin. Your very distress of mind and uneasiness of conscience is the surest sign that you have not crossed that line between God's patience and His wrath. When a man has sinned away his day of grace by committing this sin, he isn't bothered as you are. He thinks and feels that all is well, and every fear is calmed. He has no anxiety about his soul. He thinks that he is just as sure of heaven as anybody. But you are in sore distress. It is because you are still the object of the strivings of the Spirit of God. He has not ceased to strive with you. If you will come to Christ now He will in no wise cast you out. Don't let Satan keep you back from Christ any longer.

SCRIPTURAL

Although there is confusion about this sin, let us remember that there is such a sin. You cannot be saved when you like. You cannot repent and believe just when you think it time. I met a man the other day, and I was urging him to beware of committing this sin. He said, "Not now, but I will some day." I said, "How do you know that you will be saved when you come?" He said:

> "While the lamp holds out to burn,
> The greatest sinner may return."

I said, "Where did you get that?" He said, "You get that in the paraphrases." Just imagine a man risking is soul on such flimsy poetry as that. They are no more inspired than any other poem. Many are being deceived and damned along the same line today.

Let us see some of the passages.

Gen. 6: 3: "And the Lord said, MY Spirit shall not always strive with man."

Proverbs 1: 22-26: "How long, ye simple ones, will ye love simplicity? and the scorners delight in their scorning, and fools hate knowledge? Turn you at My reproof: behold, I will pour out my Spirit unto you, I will make known My words unto you.

Because I have called, and ye refused; I have stretched out My hand, and no man regarded; but ye have set at naught all my counsel, and would none of my reproof: I will also laugh at your calamity; I will mock when your fear cometh."

When your fear cometh as John the Baptist preached, and in some sense longed to meet with Christ. The day came when his desire was gratified. Pilate sent Jesus to Him, and Herod was glad, and Pilate and he became friends that day. But Herod's day of grace had come and gone. Jesus never opened His lips to him. It wasn't long after this until Herod died under the finger of the angel of God, consumed with worms. Pilate met Jesus face to face, and was sore perplexed what to do with Him. He knew in his own conscience what he should do. His wife helped him to that decision, but the mob scared him. He almost decided to release Jesus, for he asked Him, "What is truth?" But he never waited for the answer, but went and washed his hands in water, as if that relieved him from his responsibility. He sinned away his day of grace, and some years afterwards, exiled by his master, whom he tried to please, he died a suicide's death and perished. Oh! it was common then, alright.

They were just as sure of their doom that day as when it came upon them sixty years afterwards..

John 7: 34: "Ye shall seek Me and shall not find Me; and where I am, thither ye CANNOT come."

John 8: 21: "Then said Jesus again unto them, I go MY way, and ye shall seek Me and shall die in your sins; whither I go, ye CANNOT come." Verse 24: "I said therefore unto you, that ye shall die in your sins: for if ye believe not that I am HE, ye shall die in your sins."

Rom. 1: 24: "Wherefore God also gave them up to uncleanness." Verse 26: "For this cause God gave them up unto vile affections." Verse 28: "God gave them over to a reprobate mind."

Heb. 3: 12,13: "Take heed, brethren, lest there be in any of you an evil heart of unbelief, in departing from the living God. But exhort one another daily, while it is called today; lest any of you be hardened through the deceitfulness of sin."

Heb. 4: 7: "Again He limiteth a certain day, saying in David, today, after so long a time; as it is said, Today if ye will hear his voice, harden not your hearts."

Heb. 6: 4-6: "For it is impossible for those who were once enlightened, and have tasted of the heavenly gift, and were made partakers of the Holy Ghost, and have tasted of the good word of God, and the powers of the world to come, if they shall fall away, to renew them again unto repentance; seeing they crucify to themselves the Son of God afresh, and put Him to an open shame."

Heb. 10: 26-29: "For if we sin wilfully after that we have received the knowledge of the truth, there remaineth no more sacrifice for sins, but a certain looking for of judgment and fiery indignation, which shall devour the adversaries. He that despised Moses' law died without mercy under two or three witnesses: of how much sorer punishment, suppose ye, shall he be thought worthy who hath trodden under foot the Son of God, and hath counted the blood of the covenant, wherewith he was sanctified, an unholy thing, and hath done despite unto the Spirit of Grace."

2 Peter 2: 20-22: "For if after they have escaped the pollutions of the world through the knowledge of the Lord and Saviour Jesus Christ, they are again entangled therein, and overcome, the latter end is worse for them than the beginning; for it had been better for them not to have known the way of righteousness, than, after they have known it, to turn from the holy commandment delivered unto them; but it is happened unto them according to the true proverb, The dog is turned to his own vomit again; and the sow that was washed to her wallowing in the mire."

I John 5: 16: "If any man see his brother sin a sin which is not unto death, he shall ask, and he shall give him life for them that sin not unto death. There is a sin unto death: I do not say that he shall pray for it."

But not only have we this clear word of God upon this matter, but we have the record of many men in the Bible who committed this sin. Some would give you the idea that there was little or nothing about this sin in the Bible at all, but you will see from the word we have already read that it has a large place in it; and now when we see the men who crossed this line, I trust it will rid you of the delusion of the devil that you can be saved any time or when you like.

Let us turn to some of the men who crossed the dead line mentioned in the Bible.

MEN WHO COMMITTED THIS SIN

The Word of God not only gives us words of warning, but incidents of men who committed this sin. Pharaoh was dealt with by God, and he said, "Who is God that I should obey Him?" Twelve times God sent His servant to him, until God refused to deal with him any more, only in judgment.

BALAAM

Balaam was a preacher. He prophesied the coming of the Lord. You say, "Can a man be a preacher and commit this sin?" I am not saved because I am a preacher; I am a preacher because I am saved. A man may be a preacher and yet unsaved. He may have gifts and not grace. Three times God dealt with Balaam. The first time in a broad place where it was not hard for Balaam to elude God. The second time God met him in a narrow place, and before Balaam managed to get rid of God his foot was crushed. The last time God dealt with him, God pressed him so that he could not pass, but Balaam dealt deceitfully with God, and God said, "Go." And Balaam went out from God as a wandering star, to whom is reserved the blackness of darkness for ever. Take care, friend, that God is not dealing with you for the last time.

NOAH'S HELPERS

Noah believed and obeyed God and built an ark. He had many helpers during the 120 years but they would not believe, although Noah preached to them for 120 years. The day came when they were ordered into the ark, but refused, and that Unseen Hand shut the door. The rains and floods came and all were lost. Their last chance had come, and they refused. You may be a church officer, a Sunday School teacher, a singer in the choir, an active Christian worker, helping to advance Christ's Kingdom, and yet be unsaved, and when the judgment of God comes, be engulfed and damned.

JUDAS

Judas forsook all and followed Christ. It wasn't fashionable then. It involved a good deal of suffering and loss. When it came to the close of Christ's earthly ministry, Jesus said to him over the communion table, "What you are doing, do quickly." Judas looked into those eyes of love and rose up from the table and went out; and as John records the scene, he writes with a shudder, "It was night." And the light never dawned upon his doomed and darkened spirit again. Take care. You have sat at the Lord's table and kissed Him again and again. Oh, take care, take care. If you refuse to repent and believe, it may be recorded of you, "He went out and it was night," and the light of Christ's Gospel never again lighten and warn your doomed and damned spirit.

PILATE

Pilate played with Christ and conscience until Christ stood silent in his presence, and Pilate sinned away his day of grace; and history tells us that he died by his own hand in exile. His body lies in a suicide's grave and his soul in a suicide's hell.

HEROD

Herod tried to turn the Son of God into a county fair buffoon, and thought he would perform some tricks to amuse him. He died by the touch of the angel of God blaspheming God. These are cases recorded for our warning; I pray you may not go on in sin, expecting to be saved when you like.

"There is a time we know not when,
A place we know not where,
That seals the destiny of men
For glory or despair.
There is a line by us unseen
That crosses every path,
The hidden boundary between
God's patience and His wrath.

To cross that line it is to die,
To die as if by stealth,
It does not dull the beaming eye
Or pale the glow of health.
The conscience may be still at ease
The spirit light and gay;
That which is pleasing, still may please,
And fears be thrust away.

But on the forehead God has set
Indelibly a mark,
Unseen by man, for man as yet
Is blind and in the dark.
But angels know the fatal sign
And tremble at the sight,
And devils trace the lurid line
With desperate delight.

And yet the doomed man's path below,
Like Eden may have bloomed;
He does not, will not, feel or know
Or think that he is doomed.
He thinks he feels that all is well,
And every fear is calmed;
He lives, he dies, he wakes in hell
Not only doomed, but damned.

Oh, where is this mysterious bourne
By which our path is crossed,
Beyond which God Himself hath sworn
That he who goes is lost?
How far may we go on in sin?
How long will God forbear?
Where does hope end, and where begin
The confines of despair?

An answer from the skies is sent:
"Ye that from God depart,
While it is called 'Today' 'repent
And harden not your heart.'"

FOUR QUESTIONS

There are four questions I will try to answer concerning the Unpardonable Sin:

First, **What is the nature of this sin?**
Second, **Who usually commits this sin?**
Third, **What are the symptoms of one who has committed this sin?**
Fourth, **Why is it an unpardonable sin?**

ITS NATURE

You will notice from the words of the Lord that it is no ordinary sin. He says, "All manner of sin and blasphemy shall be forgiven unto men, but ..." However many or great your sins may be, there is pardon with the Lord for every one of them, but for this sin - there is no forgiveness here or hereafter. A young man came to me after one of our meetings and said, "I have committed the Unpardonable Sin." He looked as if he had, too, for he was the very picture of sorrow. I said to him, "Tell me what sin you have committed, or what have you done that makes you think that you have committed this sin?" He said, "I have broken the seventh commandment." "Well, supposing you have, and I am not making light of your sin, but listen to the words of Christ, 'ALL MANNER of sin' shall be forgiven unto men." Surely this includes the sin you mention, too?" Thank God, he saw the light. I remember another man coming to me and saying he had committed this sin. He, too, looked as if he had, for the look of the man scared me. His hair was long and unkempt, his beard long and filthy and his face dirty and bloated, his clothes greasy and dirty. He was the picture of incarnate sin and iniquity. He told me he had been brought up in the Highlands of Scotland. His father was a godly man and an elder of the church. The family respected in the district. He was fond of poaching, and one night, while out on the moors, he suddenly came upon the gamekeeper and without thinking he took the butt-end of his rifle and killed. He got twenty years for manslaughter. He told me that he never knew a day or night that he couldn't feel the blood of that man on his hands and face. He had been out of gaol for five years and never been sober, trying to drown the scene, but all in vain. He told me there was no hope for him. "I have committed the unpardonable sin." I turned him to the word of the Lord, "ALL MANNER of sin ... shall be forgiven unto men." Murder or any other sin, but this sin mentioned here shall be

forgiven. He got the light and entered into peace through believing. No, no, it isn't that, great and all as that sin is. When I
was a young man serving my time at sea, we had a third mate on
that vessel. He was an awful blasphemer, and never cursed ex-
cept in the name of the Holy Ghost. He could make the blood
run cold in your veins. We used to say, in our ignorance, that he
had committed the Unpardonable Sin. Oh, no, for when we
read these words of the Lord we see that "all manner of sin and
BLASPHEMY shall be forgiven unto men." It is just as big a sin
to take the name of God or Jesus in vain as it is to take the name
of the Holy Ghost in vain. So that isn't the sin.

In its nature it is against the Holy Ghost. Many times it is
recorded that the Pharisees attributed the power of Christ to
the devil. They said He cast out devils by the Prince of the
Devils. He revealed His deity and the truth of His mission and
message by the life He lived, and by the words He spake, and
the miracles He performed. He said, "Believe me for the work's
sake." But in spite of this evidence they denied Him. Have we
any sin like this today? When men deny His deity and make light
of His authority, and try to make out that the word of God is not
infallible; when they attribute the Spirit's power to the power of
man; or when they make light of the necessity of regeneration
and say that all man needs is a better environment or better
knowledge. Take care, man, that you don't commit this sin. You
are on tender ground. In its nature it is wilful and deliberate.
They made up their minds about Him. They held council meetings about Him, and what they would do with Him, and they
wilfully and deliberately rejected Him. You have again and again
resisted the strivings of the Spirit. You have stifled His voice.
You have quenched the burning convictions He set alight in you.
You have a hard time doing all this. Take care you don't succeed
in sinning away your day of grace and damning your soul. It is
also in its nature a sin against clearest Gospel light. It is not a
sin of ignorance. The Lord said, "And whosoever speaketh a word

against the Son of Man, it shall be forgiven him" That is, they might have mistaken His deity because of His humanity. If they did they would be forgiven, for it was on account of their ignorance. His deity was veiled by His humanity. He would allow for that; but to deny the open Heaven and the descending dove; to deny the voice from Heaven saying, "This is My beloved Son in whom I am well pleased" - to doubt that was to shut their eyes to the light. To deny the miracle of His sinless and unique life and the manifestations of divine power in His miracles, was to seal their doom and ensure their damnation. Friends, if it was possible in that dim, dark distant day to commit this sin, how much more possible in this day of such light and privilege, with the light of two thousand years shining on and from that life. You have been raised in the lap of Christianity, and yet you shut your eyes to the light. Take heed; to continue to do so is to succeed in sinning away your day of grace and damning your soul.

KICKING OUT THE LIGHT

It is a law of Nature that what you do not use you lose. The faculty that God gave you, and gives every human creature when he is born, will surely atrophy and wither away if not used; and there comes a time when you would long to be able to perceive and believe, but you have lost the power by non-use. A collector of stalactites heard of wonderful specimens to be had in one of the Mammoth Caves of Kentucky, but the access to the cave was difficult and dangerous. He determined to have a try. So he tied a cord on the outside of the cave, and with a candle made his way in, paying out the cord as he entered. At last he succeeded in getting to the place. The sight of such specimens excited him. He carelessly laid down the light and cord and began to gather the specimens. In his excitement he kicked the light out. He was dazed for a time, and then began to search for the cord. His friends missed him for many days, but could not find him, until one happened to see the cord, and knowing his friend's hobby, immediately suspected where he was. He got another friend, and they both followed the cord until they came to the cave. What a sight met their gaze! There was the decomposing corpse of their friend, and some few inches away from his hands was the end of the cord. They could trace the marks where he had groped and crawled hour after hour, around the cave, searching for the cord. To find it meant life, sunshine and friends. He groped in vain. Oh, the agony of that man's mind! How he would bewail his carelessness! How eagerly he would long and look for the cord! It was all in vain. He perished. There may come a day in your life if you continue resisting the Holy Spirit, when you will seek and not find, when you will call aloud for mercy and no response. How you will bewail your sinful and wilful folly! Oh, beware; do not kick the light out in groping for life's pleasures and possessions.

> "Light obeyed increaseth light;
> Light resisted bringeth night;
> Who shall give me will to choose
> If the love of light I lose?
> Speed my soul, this instant yield
> Let the light its sceptre wield;
> While thy God prolongs His grace,
> Haste thee to His Holy Face."

THE GUILTY ONES

The people who usually are guilty of this sin are the religious and respectable ones. It was the elite of religious society in the days of our Lord's flesh who committed it. There is more danger of the one who has had privilege and opportunity than the one who has had little or none. "Woe unto thee, Chorazin.

Woe unto thee, Bethsaida." Why? Because they have been exalted with privilege and opportunity. Is this not true of many here? Yet in spite of all this, you have rejected His call and claim, or courteously ignored them. "How shall we escape if we neglect?" A sin-seared conscience is an awful thing. Take heed lest we be hardened through the deceitfulness of sin. The Gospel either softens or hardens. It is either a saver of life or of death. The wax is melted by the fire, the clay is hardened. So with the Gospel in its action upon us. If we resist the Spirit we become hardened, until there comes a time when every approach of the Spirit toward us is useless. Better never to have been born than to allow yourself to become hardened by your continued resistance to the Holy Spirit.

SYMPTOMS

The symptoms are definite and clear in the one who has succeeded in sinning away his day of grace. They may not all be evident at the one time and in the one person. There is no response to the Gospel Message. If I sound out the thunders of Sinai, you deride and call me antiquated and fanatical. There is no fear or dread. If I sound out the silvery wooing notes of Calvary, you are pleased and continue to presume upon the mercy of God by rejecting Christ and remaining in your sins. Golgotha's rocks rent asunder when our Lord was dying, and when they heard His dying wail, "MY God, MY God why hast thou forsaken Me?" But your adamantine heart was never broken. Why? You have sinned away your day of grace.

Another symptom: There is no recognition of need. You wrap yourself around in carnal security and smug complacency, and persuade yourself and try to persuade others that you are all right. You say, "Well, I do my best to live a good life. I go to church, say prayers, pay my dues, and live honestly." Say, friend, would you dare to offer the already condemned deeds of the body for the sin of your soul? It is the blood that atones for the soul. God says, "When I see the blood I will pass over you." Not when I see your earnestness, zeal or religiosity, or morality; but the blood. What daring insult to God to substitute your deeds for the precious blood of Christ; the filthy rags of your righteousness for the seamless, spotless robe of Christ's righteousness. A true child of God despairs of every virtue or merit, only the merit and virtue of his Saviour. He works out his own salvation with fear and trembling, but you have nothing but a false, presumptuous, blasphemous confidence. Why is this? You have spurned God's remedy for sin until the offer has been withdrawn from you.

Then another symptom: There is no repentance on account of sin. You are only sorry for your sin when it is found out. You laugh and mock at sin. You revel and riot in it. The child of God is in the pains of hell and great sorrow and heaviness of spirit when conscious of sin, and never rests until he has come under the cleansing power of the peace-speaking blood of Christ. You make light of your sin and laugh at it.

Another symptom is: There is no realisation of danger. You laugh at hell as if it were not a reality, or as if you were not on the way there. How can you? Others by your side are in great fear, even horror, because of their danger. You have no such feeling. You sit unmoved and often asleep, under every appeal. The accidents and deaths around you are warnings falling upon deaf ears. Yet if you were to die now, you would be damned in hell for all eternity, but you do not realise it. Even when some come to die they have no bands in their death. They die fearless, but none the less doomed and damned. Who would think that hell is opening under your feet, and there is only a step between you and damnation. It is an awful state to be in - to have no concern about your danger.

I mention another symptom: Bitter rage against the Gospel and Gospel preachers. What cruel and unjust things some of you have been saying about me! Have I told lies? Have I deceived you? Have I not been true to your soul? You know I have declared the whole counsel of God without fear or favour. Why, then, are you angry? Others have been led to repentance and submission, and others have been confirmed in their faith, but you are only more embittered and enraged. This is always the result of sinning against the Holy Ghost. Are any of these symptoms in your life? If you are in some measure tender of conscience, I beseech you, repent and believe.

WHY UNPARDONABLE?

Why is this sin unpardonable? Is there not virtue in the blessed blood of Christ? Can God not forgive? Listen, there must always be two parties in forgiveness, the forgiver and the one to be forgiven. If the one needing forgiveness will not receive it or be forgiven, then he cannot be forgiven - not that there was no forgiveness but he refused it. Friend, God has forgiven you, and offers forgiveness to you now, and He has been doing so all along, but you have deliberately and wilfully rejected or ignored it. How can you be forgiven if you will not?

The unpardonable sin is the continued and obstinate rejection of Christ until there comes a time when His Spirit ceases to strive and the offer of mercy and forgiveness is withdrawn, and you are left to your doom and damnation. I most lovingly and earnestly entreat you, who are not impervious to this appeal, but feel your need and danger, do not refuse God's offer of forgiveness, but confess and forsake your sins, and He will forgive, sanctify and glorify. I feel there are some here now who are on the verge of yielding. How I wish I could help you to yield now! If I dismiss the service and leave, your conversation may take away your impressions, and you will harden your conscience and endanger your soul. But if you could be led to decide now while you are awakened and alarmed, by any act of mine, how gladly I will do it.

GOD'S HAND UPON YOU

I fear to let you go. I feel like the nurse in a hospital during the Civil War. A young lad had his arm and shoulder fearfully shattered by a shell. They did their best for him, but the limb and body were so shattered that they could not very securely tie up the arteries. The nurse was given orders to see that the wounded lad was not allowed to move. The nurse sat by his bed as he moaned and talked in his delirium. Toward morning he quieted down. One of the other patients demanded her services and she thought, as the lad was so quiet, she could leave him and attend to the others. When she returned she discovered to her horror, that the lad had moved and the blood was oozing through the bandages and bed to the floor. She stripped off the bandages and seizing the artery, sent for the physician. When he came he said she might as well let go, as he must die. Nothing could be done. The bleeding had brought the lad to consciousness, and he heard the doctor's words of doom. Looking up into the nurse's face he pleaded with her not to let go, as he was unfit and unready to die. He had run away from mother and home. She turned away her head, and when she looked again he had gone into eternity. God has placed you under my hand today. You are conscious of your danger. I have my hand still upon you. Will you not now decide? Oh, I pray you, do not delay. I cannot hold you much longer. I pray God that my letting you go now may not mean your death and damnation.

> Sinner, how thy heart is troubled.
> God is drawing very near.
> Do not hide thy deep emotion
> Do not check that falling tear.
> Come at once accept His mercy -
> He is waiting - come today.
> Oh, be saved; His grace is free!
> Oh, be saved; He died for thee.

The Great Judgment Day

❖

"And as it is appointed unto men once to die, but after this the judgment." - Hebrews 9: 27

An old Civil War veteran lay dying. His minister came to see him, and as he sat by the bedside of the dying old warrior he wondered what he might say, or wondered what way he might say it; so he said, "John, are you afraid to die?" The old man raised himself up on his elbow and looked with anger and indignation at the minister, and said, "Look here, sir; I have faced death many a time, on many a bloody battlefield, and never was frightened; I have faced it many a time since, and do you think, now that I have come to the last of life, I'll be scared? I'm no coward, and I dare you to insult me in my dying hour." He fell back on his pillow exhausted. The minister was taken all aback for a time, and wondered what he might say now. After lifting his heart to the Lord he said, "John are you prepared for what comes after death?" "Oh," he said, "that is what makes me scared."

GOODBYE GOD

How many there are like him! It isn't the thought or fact of death that scares them, Many a man has faced death with a laugh on bloody battlefields, but when they think about what comes after death, there isn't a man who is not scared.

CURIOSITY ABOUT THE FUTURE

Isn't it strange how men and women will go to this one and the other, and pay large sums of money, if only they can tell them something about the future? There is that in every one of us that likes to pry into the unknown. That is why spiritualism prospers so well these days, and gypsies and palmists and other emissaries of the devil, with their delusions. People believe their lies, and yet doubt the Word of God. You don't need to go to these frauds, for they are just as wise as you are about the future. You have the Bible in your hand. Go to it, and there you will find accurately all about what comes after death. What is it comes after death? It is judgment. "And as it is appointed unto men once to die, but after this the judgment."

I want to speak to you tonight about the Judgment. It is strange the amount of confusion there is in the minds of many about this subject. Some of our hymns are the source of this confusion, I believe. Many seem to have a notion that there will be one great Judgment Day, when good and bad, saved and unsaved, sheep and goats, will be gathered around the Throne of judgment. This is not scriptural; for the Bible clearly teaches that there is not only one judgment, but there are four. You can see what confusion there will be if we do not get to see this clearly. Let me try to set them forth in order.

FOUR JUDGMENTS

The Judgment of Sin, which has passed for the believer, Christ having been judged for his sins, and he himself "crucified with Christ." Hence, "He that believeth shall not come into judgment." This judgment took place when the Lord Jesus died on the cross on Calvary, more than nineteen centuries ago. Many of God's dear children are kept in bondage to fear, and have no peace with God, through the supposition that they have yet to be judged for their sin. Such is not the case, blessed be God. For Christ has been judged in their place - "has appeared to put away sin by the sacrifice of Himself" - and the Holy Ghost says, "Your sins and iniquities will I remember no more." Moreover, the believer is "perfected for ever" and "shall not come into judgment." All my iniquities were laid on Him - not some of them. All my past and present and future sins have been settled by Jesus when He died on Calvary. The sin question is **for ever** settled for the believer. If this is not so, then every time a believer sins Christ must die or else he will, for God never forgives sin. He forgives the sinner. He always hates sin, and deals in judgment with it. Even when sin was on His Beloved Son He could not look on Him with complacency, but struck Him in judgment until He cried out, "My God, My God, why hast Thou forsaken Me." The work is finished perfectly.

The second judgment that will take place may take place at any moment - at this moment. Glory to God! - the judgment of the Redeemed of all ages, when each shall receive his own reward, according to his own labour after they have been caught up to meet the Lord in the air, in their glorified bodies. This will take place before the "judgment seat of Christ." Believers "must all appear before the judgment seat of Christ" to "receive reward" or "suffer loss," according to their works on earth. It will not be a question of heaven or hell, since they are all previously in heaven in "bodies of glory," but of what reward, if any, they are to get when there. Paul has been with Christ - so has the dying thief - for hundreds of years. How absurd it is then to suppose it has yet to be decided whether they are fit to be there! If we live here as believers, worldly, pleasure-loving, selfish lives, it will be like hay, wood and stubble, and when the fire hits it, it will go up in a puff of smoke; but if we have lived for the Lord and done our best to win souls, then it will be like gold, silver, precious stones, that will endure the fire and be to our reward and God's glory through all eternity. There are different degrees of glory in heaven, as there are different degrees of torment in hell. I don't know anything like this truth for inspiring one in this life to be out and out for the Lord. How many that day will have only faded leaves instead of ripened fruit.

The third judgment to take place is the judgment of the **Living Nations** on the earth, divided like sheep and goats, according to their treatment of the faithful Jewish "Remnant", whom the Lord calls "my brethren". This will take place at the commencement of the Millennium, or Christ's reign of 1,000 years, in the valley of Jehoshaphat, at the base of the Mount of Olives. By a careful study of Matthew 25: 31-46, and a comparison with Joel 3: 3-16, and with Zechariah 14: 1-9, it will be seen that this judgment is confined to the Living Nations (Gentiles) on the earth, when the Lord Jesus returns to reign. This is important to grasp, as it is generally confounded with the fourth judgment which take s place at least 1,000 years later.

The fourth and last judgment is the subject I wish to take up with you today - the judgment of the 'Unconverted Dead'. This takes place after the close of the Millennium or Christ's reign of 1,000 years, before the great White Throne, after the earth and heaven have fled away. This judgment is confined to the only remaining class, viz., the unconverted dead of all ages, who are condemned to their awful doom in the Lake of Fire for eternity.

WHICH JUDGMENT?

Your decision today may determine what judgment you will be at in eternity. If you accept Him now as your personal Saviour you will never come to the judgment of the great White Throne, but you will be judged for the deeds done in the body as a believer at the Judgment Seat of Christ; but if you reject Him, then, just as sure as God has said it, you will appear before the great White Throne of pure unadulterated justice and judgment.

Your decision today will determine which resurrection you will be at - whether the first resurrection unto everlasting glory, or the second resurrection unto eternal perdition and damnation.

There are four things I want to say today concerning judgment.

First - **The Certainty of this Judgment**
Second - **The Day itself**
Third - **The Judge**
Fourth - **Who are the judged?**

CERTAINTY OF JUDGMENT

Judgment is going on on every hand today. You cannot violate any law of nature without suffering for it now. Nature never forgives; she demands the utmost farthing every time and all the time. There is no mercy in the sun, or the moon, or the stars, or anywhere in nature, but in God. Our hospitals are filled with men and women who are paying for their sins, or the sins of others, but they are suffering in judgment.

Put your finger in the fire and it will burn you. Lie, and you become a liar. Steal, and you become a thief. While there will be future judgment, still there is judgment, going on right now, for "whatsoever a man soweth, that shall he also reap," and more than he sowed, too; but everyone of us will reap **if we sow**. There is nothing surer than this. You may deny or doubt the fact of coming judgment, but you cannot deny or doubt the fact of it now. There are men today and they are suffering the tortures of hell for one night's debauchery. You can make up your mind that you will suffer if you sin, and suffer here as well as hereafter. It makes sinning easy for some; for they think that the judgment day is far ahead, that it has lost its terror for them, and they think it mightn't be true; so they can sin with an easy conscience and light spirit. Don't forget there is a harvest going on **now**. But I am also sure there is a judgment day coming, for common sense demands one. In every civilised land here you have justice of some sort of another. Even amongst the lowest races there is some sort of sense that demands justice. They try their law breakers and deal with them. It is more so in civilised lands. We have our various courts and judges and law officers. Why? Because we demand judgment or justice. You couldn't get a couple of men fighting, who do not demand from each other a square deal, and the crowd that gathers sees they get it. It is in us, that 'something' that cries out for judgment. Where did we get that? We got that from the One who created us. Has He created us like that and He Himself devoid of it? Just as sure as we feel like this, so God will see there is judgment by and by.

Do you mean to tell me that there is no judgment for the distiller and brewer, the publicans and spirit merchants? - these pariahs who are fattening on the ruin of their species. Every penny they have is stained with blood and tears. Their prosperity has been the ruin of their fellows. They thrived on ruined homes, broken hearts, blighted lives, starving children, and damned souls.

Although licensed by the Government, do you think that this will stop God from dealing with them in judgment? Nay, verily. Just as sure as God lives, they will give an account for every tear shed, and every throb of pain felt by poor women and mothers for the cry of starving children for bread; and as God dealt with Pharaoh in judgment for his treatment of His people, so God will deal with these monsters, who can live in luxury while their victims live and die in misery. Is there no judgment for the moral leper who ruins young women and sacrifices them on the altar of lust and then runs away with a laugh and evades the law here? It seems to me that such a rascal is too bad for hell itself; but just as sure as God lives, he will bring him into judgment. Is there to be no judgment for the man or woman, who won't give up their Church or the world, but will, by their worldliness ruin the Church? Is Judas the only one to go 'to his own place'? Can men today sin with impunity in the Church, and because they are there will they escape the wrath of God? Judas sold Jesus for a decent price, but the Judases today don't think Him worthy of even that; but they will sit down at His table and take the oath of loyalty and love, and then go right out and sell Him for a glass of whisky or a game of cards, or a dance or picture show or theatre. They do more to hurt the Church than all the sinners on the outside of her; in fact, they keep them out because of their inconsistencies and worldliness, and do you think there will be no judgment of them? If God damned Ananias and Sapphira when they lied to the Holy Ghost, has He lost the power to   execute judgment today? I would a million times rather meet God out of the Church as meet Him in judgment as a Church member who played the hypocrite or the Judas Iscariot. Is there no judgment for the minister who can stand in the pulpit, and in the name of scholarship or for the sake of notoriety deny the inspiration of the Bible and the deity and authority of Christ and thus ruin the faith of many and hurt the Church bought with His blood? Or the theological professor who robs young men of the faith of their fathers and turns them out ministerial infidels? I would far rather a man inoculated my boy with some deadly disease and sent him to his grave than have any man rob him of his faith in God and God's Word. The sad thing is that these men are living on the funds of orthodox people. They have neither the morality nor decency to leave their lucrative jobs and come out and earn an honest living. If they have lost faith in what the Church stands for and believes in and what they are paid to teach, let them do this and everybody will have respect for them and feel sorry for them; but while they hold down their jobs at the sacrifice of morality, then they are outside the respect and sympathy and support of every believing man - or ought to be. But just as sure as God lives and has said it, they will stand before Him in that day and give an account to Him for the young men and women whose faith they have ruined. What a day that will be! I would rather meet God as a highwayman than as one who robbed men of their faith and damned their souls. Men may escape judgment here from man, but none can escape from God. In the midst of all the ruin, pain, injustice, and hypocrisy that abounds today in spite of the law of the land and God, this one thought brings peace and comfort: that God will bring everyone into judgment, where there will be pure unadorned justice.

THE BIBLE TEACHES IT

But supposing we had none of these reasons for believing that there will be a Judgment Day, we have the sure Word of God and that settles it for many of us. No man can go to the Bible and not be convinced there is a judgment. It seems to me that a man must have a queer notion of the Lord Jesus when he thinks that He is all love and not justice. I could not trust a God like that. A minister said to an old Scottish saint as she lay dying, "What is it gives you comfort in your dying hour? Is it the love of God?" "Oh, no," she said. He was surprised and said, "Is it the mercy of God?" "No," she said again; "I have no right to either His love or mercy." "Then, what is it gives you comfort in your dying hour?" "It is the righteousness of God," she said for, "He is just, and the justifier of everyone that believeth." God is not a capricious God. God is stern, inexorable, just as well as loving; and if you will not bend, you will break, if you will not turn, you will burn. Hear God's word, "Rejoice, O young man in thy youth; and let thine heart cheer thee in the days of thy youth, and walk in the ways of thine heart, and in the sight of thine eyes: but know thou that for all these things God will bring thee into judgment." Again, "God shall bring every work into judgment, with every secret thing, whether it be good or evil." "God hath appointed a day in which he shall judge the world." God thrust out Adam and Eve when they fell. God branded Cain after he killed his brother. God drowned a world with flood, and burnt up the cities of the plain, and overthrew many nations on account of their sin. Has he changed today? Is He scared to execute judgment on man because this is, "Man's Day?" You would almost think He was by the way men live and talk today. But He says, "I am the Lord, I change not; therefore ye sons of Jacob are not consumed." An infidel dying said, "I could die in peace if I could believe the Bible wasn't true." Some of you could live in sin easier if you could believe this, too; but just as sure as you live and God lives, you will be brought into judgment if you don't repent and believe now. Turn from the notions of men and from your own notions, and take the Word of God for what you believe. You will find it safer here and hereafter

JUDGMENT IS APPOINTED

What kind of a day with the Judgment Day be? We are told in the Word of God, it will be an appointed day. "God hath appointed a day in which He will judge the world in righteousness." There is no luck with God, there is no chance, as people talk about; there is no accident with God; there is no evasion. God has appointed a day in which He will judge the world in righteousness. Many a man overtaken in crime who has been let out on bail has cleared the country and evaded judgment. Brother you may be very smart and you may evade every judgment of your land, and you may clear out from every court of justice in your land, but here is one that you will not get rid of. God's appointments are always kept. God appointed the seasons - spring, summer, autumn, winter and you never heard of them failing. God appointed night and day and you never heard of a day when the sun forgot to rise. God appointed these heavenly bodies and you never heard of them going wrong did you? I once sailed for five months and nineteen days and never saw land, and yet so regularly did the sun rise and set that we reached our desired haven in perfect safety and, if in natural things God's appointments are kept, He will be just as faithful in keeping this one, whether you like it or not; whether you are willing or not; whether you are young or old. Thus saith the Lord, "If ye can break My covenant of the day and My covenant of the night, and that there should not be day and night in their season, then may also My covenant be broken." When God's appointed day comes you will keep that appointment. You will not be able to get a substitute then; there will be no excuses accepted. God's appointments are made to be kept, and He will make sure that they are kept.

THIS IS MAN'S DAY

There is a great day coming - Christ's day. But 'this is man's day,' and a wonderful day it is - a day of inventions, a day of improvements, but it is man's day.

"Our Lord is now rejected,
And by the world disowned;
By the many still neglected,
And by the few enthroned.
But soon He'll come in glory
The hour is drawing nigh,
For the Judgment Day is coming
By and by."

Take your innings, brother; this is your day. You can spit in His face today, you can trample His blood under your feet today, you can mock Him to His face. Go ahead; it is a short day at best you have got; take it. His day is coming. He is the Man of Sorrows today; He is the bleeding, tender, gentle Saviour today. That day, He will be the crowned Christ; He will be clothed with glory and majesty. It will be His day. Your day will have ended. Today you may laugh Him to scorn, ridicule His claims, mock His kingdom and cross, but His day is coming when every enemy will be under His feet and you will be there if you continue rejecting.

DAY OF WRATH

And not only is it Christ's day, it is a day of wrath. Thank God, this is a day of grace. There is not one single doubt about that, it is a day of grace today. But man, when the Judgment Day dawns upon your dark and doomed spirit you will cry out, and from that anguished heart of yours will rise a most agonising prayer, but there is no mercy. Mercy is ended; the day of grace is gone; the Judgment has begun. Wrath and fiery indignation are at that great White Throne; your prayers and your tears will be unavailing there. Your anguish will have no effect then. You will stand before the Christ you are mocking today.

THE LAST DAY

And then we are told it will be the last day. Time will have ceased; the great bell and the knell of your time will have sounded; saints will be in everlasting and celestial bliss and glory, and you will stand at that pure White Throne to be judged and then damned through all eternity. No time again; all time gone; and the eternal ages beginning to roll. Thank God, you are in time today, and in the day of grace.

THE JUDGE

Who is the Judge? I want to say several things concerning this Judge, Jesus Christ. It is a good thing to know the judge before whom you will be tried.

In England there used to be a judge whom they called the "Hanging Judge" and there was not a criminal in the land but who feared going before him. He dealt out justice, and he got most of the criminal cases to try. The Judge you will meet in that day is omnipresent; His eyes run to and fro throughout all the earth; He is everywhere. And when you stand at the Great White Throne of Justice that Judge will be able to say, "I was there when you did it; the darkness could not hide it from Me." The judges of our land, although many of them are wise men, often make mistakes, but there will be no wrong condemnation then. Many a time a judge in our day has to condemn a man on circumstantial evidence, but not so with Jesus. You will stand in the presence of One before Whom you lived your life. Every thought He knows, ever feeling He understands, everything you did and everywhere you went, however dark or secret, He was there.

An infidel was lying on his bed dying, and he thought he would like to see his little daughter (she had been sent away to school) before he died, and the daughter came; but she did not seem to realise the condition her father was in, and she began to tell how well she was getting on at school. He pointed over to a card on the wall and asked her to read, and it was this: "God is nowhere." She read, "G-o-d God, i-s is, n-o-w now, h-e-r-e, here." And that poor man tried to shut out God. You cannot get away from Him. He is the unavoidable Christ. You were never in a bar but He was there. You were never in any bed of sin, but He was there. **He is omnipresent**. He is everywhere.

He is omniscient. That is, not only is He every where present, but He is perfect in knowledge, and when you stand in His presence and look in His face and when judgment is passed upon you, you will say, "Lord that is true, perfectly true." Perfect in knowledge. All the judges in our land are limited in their knowledge, but here is the One before whom you are going to stand who is all-wise and knows everything perfectly.

And the last thing I want to say about the Judge is this: **He is omnipotent**; almighty; not only everywhere, not only all-wise, but all-powerful. I have been in South America, South Africa and other parts of the world, and I have sat and worked with men who have evaded the law of their land. If they went back to England, the law would grip them immediately; and there they are in other countries, evading the law. Why? Because the law is not almighty. It is mighty, but not almighty. There are men in your country today and if the law could only catch them it would bring them to justice. The old Puritans used to say, in their quaint way, that "Though God should burn the world, He would sift the ashes and bring ever sinner into judgment." "Rejoice, O young man in thy youth and let thy heart cheer thee in the days of thy youth and walk in the ways of thine heart, and in the sight of thine eyes, but know thou that for all these things God will bring thee into judgment."

You may mock God and deride Him to His face today. I heard a man stand up and say, "If there is a God, let Him strike me dead in five minutes' time," as if that would be any evidence there was a God. You may brazen God to His face, but, brother, there is a time coming when He will break you. You will not bend to His pleading and love today, but when He grips you, you will break. His arm is strong to save. It will be just as strong to bring you to judgment then, and, although you might evade every judge and all earthly judges, you will never evade this Judge, for He is almighty.

THE JUDGED

Who are the judged? "They whose names were not written in the Lamb's Book of Life were cast into the lake of fire." Although your name is on the communion roll of your Church, though you are living a very moral and good life, and are a professor of religion but not a vital possessor of life, having a form of godliness, but denying its power, my dear brothers, whenever the end comes you will stand at the Great White Throne of Justice and from there be cast into the lake of fire. Drunkards and murderers, harlots and blasphemers, as well as rich and poor, the moral and the pure and religious, all will stand there. It does not matter how good a moral life you may have lived, it does not matter how many prayers you may have uttered, it does not matter how much money you may have given to the poor, how strenuously you may have wrought for social reform, if your name has not been written in the Lamb's Book of Life, then you will stand at that Great White Throne to be judged and damned.

MERCY STILL

I do not know how you may feel, but these are awful things for any man to have to say, and if I studied my own heart and my own feelings I would not talk of them. I cherish the love of God as well as any man. It thrills and fires my heart as nothing else can; but I would be untrue to you if I did not tell you the other side. It is the love of God that reveals the other side, and, my dear brother, if you will not repent, if you will not seek the Lord, if you will not turn to Jesus Christ in this day of grace, you must meet Him in judgment. You have the option of meeting Him in grace today, but you will not have the option of meeting Him that day; you must. Thank God, that Great White Throne is still vacant. There is another throne, bloodstained and crimson - a throne of grace whereby we may obtain mercy and find grace to help in every time of need. Dear man, you will not rush into the judgment, will you? Will you not be wise today and come to the throne of grace, crimson with His blood, and obtain mercy? There is great mercy with the Lord, although you have trampled this blood under foot for years. Although you may have raked in the very kennels of hell, there is mercy with the Lord.

RECONCILIATION

In the North of England there was a family - one of the most respectable and respected families, and one of the oldest families in the country. They had only one boy and when he grew up to years of responsibility he developed habits of gambling and drinking. His father was a Christian man and a Member of Parliament for that district. The son, by his drunken habits brought his name to shame and disgrace. His father had again and again redeemed him, paid his debts and got him out of trouble; but at last, broken hearted, he said, "John, if you stop this life and live as you ought to live, this home is yours. But if you intend to live as you have been living, I have paid your debts for the last time. There is the door." And the young fellow picked up his hat and left the home.

A father is not like a mother, and although the father grew impatient, the mother's love was never exhausted. She became sad-hearted and faded away, and in spite of all that was done to lift her spirits, she sank into decline. They took her to physician after physician, and from health resort to health resort, and after years of trouble and expense she came home to die. The doctor said, "Madam, I fear you will pass away today." And when the doctor came out the husband said, "Well?" And the doctor said, "This is her last day here." The husband went to his wife's bedside. She was lying there white and weak and with her emaciated hands she took his hand and said, "You know what is bringing me to a premature grave. I am dying, and would like to look into the face of my child once more. Oh, grant me this dying request. My heart is hungry, withered and broken; but now it is the end. John; I will never have another petition to ask; but I would like to see my boy, to look on his face again before I die. It would ease my deathbed and make it bright."

They discovered the boy was in Newcastle-on-Tyne, and they wired for him. He got the wire, and almost with a broken heart he read the message. You will find a tender heart under many a prodigal's breast. I have many a time sat yonder in the Salvation Army barracks at Mafeking in South Africa, with the tears running down my cheeks. Though we would not listen to the preaching, we used to listen to the singing, and there was one woman who used to sing:

> "Your mother still prays for you, Jack,
> Your mother still prays for you, Jack,
> In that land far away o'er the ocean,
> Your mother still prays for you."

I have seen three hundred of us sitting their sobbing; we all had good mothers. When this young fellow got the wire telling him his mother was dying, it seemed as if the trains were too slow; and when he came to the door he did not knock, he did not need to ask which was her room. In that bedroom he had seen the light of the world. There he had learned to pray. Once he was fair as the morning dew as he knelt at his mother's knee. But now, sin-stained and marred, he came home. Kneeling down, he began, "Oh, mother, my sin has broken your heart, is bringing you to a premature grave. My God, to think that I am the murderer of my mother! Is there forgiveness with you or with God?" And she said, "John, I have never ceased to love you. While it is true your sin and conduct have broken my heart, it is true that my love has followed you all the years; and John, if your mother never ceases to love you, and if your mother is so willing to forgive you, what must God be towards you? Oh, John, I am dying, but it seems to me I have to tell Jesus my heaven will be no heaven if you do not come there. Will you promise me, my boy, that you will meet me yonder, that you will take Christ as your Saviour tonight, and then meet mother in the realms of glory?" "Yes, mother, by the grace of God, I will follow Christ." And she turned round to her husband and said, "John, our life has been happy. God has given us this child, and now I will make another request. I want you to be reconciled to him. He has given himself to Christ, and by God's grace will never bring shame on your name again. Will you not be reconciled to your boy?" She raised herself in her bed, and taking her husband's hand in hers, and her son's hand in the other, she brought the two together in a clasp, and then fell back on her pillow a lifeless corpse. The two men, grasping each other's hands, looked in each other's eyes, and then into the face of the mother and wife, and with the tears blinding their eyes they were both reconciled over the dead mother.

Men, today will you be reconciled to God over the broken body of Jesus? He puts his nail-pierced hand out to you, and He says, "Oh, be ye reconciled to God." Will you put your hand in His and obtain mercy? God help you!

Hell

---❖---

"And in hell he lifted up his eyes, being in torments, and seeth Abraham afar off, and Lazarus in His bosom" - Luke 16:23

I am bringing this solemn subject to you tonight with no light-ness of spirit or flippancy of speech, neither is it my inten-tion to work upon your feelings or fill your heart with fear unnecessarily. Although if I can accomplish this very thing, and it makes you decide for Christ tonight, I will be the last to apolo-gise for doing so, and you will be the last to ask me to do so, for I am sure of this, that if the fear of hell brings you to Christ, it is not the fear of hell that will keep you following Christ. It will be His love and loveliness that will bind you to Him with bands stronger than steel.

Neither do I bring this message to you apologetically, for I have no apology to make for any message of my Master. Neither do I come to discuss this subject, but to declare it with all plainness and fearlessness and, I trust, in love. I believe there never was a day when this message was needed more than the day we are living in. The pulpit is almost silent about it or denies it, and the average church member treats it with contempt, as if it were some antedated and antiquated nursery bogey or fable. I do not preach it with the desire to see you go there, but with the earnest desire to warn you to flee from the wrath to come; for just as God has said it, hell is the destiny and doom of every impenitent, Christ-rejecting man or woman. I would not go the length of my foot to hear what the wisest man has to say about hell or what he thinks about it, for the opinions of the most intellectual theologian in the land today are of no more value than the opinions of the most ignorant man in the world. I am not here to give you what "I" think about hell, or what the Church thinks about hell, but what the Lord has to say about it. My reason for confining it to what Jesus says about it is because it limits the range of our inquiry and also gives authoritative evidence or knowledge about hell.

TWO REASONS

I take this subject up for two reasons.

First. For the sake of the Christians who are here, to inform their minds and arouse them to a solemn sense of their responsibility. Surely if there is a spark of humanity in us, or the love of God about us, we can never be at ease while our fellow-men are on their way to hell, and do nothing to warn them and win them for Christ. If a house were on fire tonight in this town and you knew that in that burning building there were men and women and children in danger of a horrible death, is there a man here, yea, or a woman either, who wouldn't do all in their power to save them, even at the risk of their own lives? Every man or woman worthy of the name would be eager to do this. If you knew that a boat had capsized in the bay and a number of people were drowning, which of us here would not risk his life to save them? Yet men and women every day on every side of us are rushing to hell as fast as time can take them, not to a physical death merely, but to eternal death and hell. How can we sit still and do nothing to save them? The worst of it is, not only will many who call themselves Christians do nothing to save their fellows, but they will do all they can to hinder those who are doing all they can to snatch them as brands from the burning, by criticising their methods and messages and calling them coarse and vulgar, saying they are too emotional and sensational, etc. Instead of boosting them and encouraging them, they do all they can to discourage and hinder. May the Lord use my message tonight to rouse every Christian up to do all he or she can by all means to save some.

General Booth, the founder and leader of the Salvation Army, said to some hundreds of his cadets when they were graduating from the training home: "Young men, if I had my way I would never have had you here for years in this Training Home, but I would have put you in hell for twenty-four hours, so that you might have felt the pains and pangs of the damned, that you might have heard their weeping and wailing and their gnashing of teeth, and seen something of their torments. I would then have let you out and sent you into the world to warn men and women to flee from the wrath to come. I would be sure of this, you would never take the work easy, or treat it negligently while you were in it." I feel the old general was about right. Oh! if the old devil can get us to disbelieve in the fact of hell, then he knows that he has cut the nerve of our energy and effort. I remember one time lying anchored in Table Bay, Cape Town, waiting our turn to get into dock to discharge our cargo. One evening after we all had turned in, we heard a cry so clear, "We're drowning! We're drowning!" Not a man of us but was on deck with very little clothing on him and into the boat. Maybe we didn't make those ash oars bend as we pulled for the men who were drowning. Maybe the bos'on didn't urge us on, and the men who were left behind cheer us. They didn't criticise how we pulled just as long as we pulled for all we were worth. I couldn't imagine one of the men on the vessel saying to the other men, "There is far too much excitement here." Or "They are not decently enough dressed," or "They are not rowing according to the rules." Man! if one had begun to talk like that, they would have thrown him overboard. Oh, no! They were all intent on rescuing those drowning men, and doing all they could to help those who were pulling the oars. Suppose some man had come along and said with great eloquence and intelligence, "These men are not in any danger; it is only imaginary danger or parabolic danger," or "They only think they are in danger. If they only knew better or were more perfectly informed, they would not make all that fuss." Do you think we would have done all we did in the way we did if we believed that? You know we wouldn't. It was because their danger was real that we were so eager to rescue them.

HELL A REALITY

Hell is a reality, Christian men and women. Let us be up and at it - and at it all the time.

Second. Then I bring this message to those who are not yet saved, but are on their way to hell, so that they may get awakened to their danger tonight and urged to flee from the wrath to come. It is awful to think that you sit there in your sin, and if you died right now, in hell you would lift up your eyes, being in torment for eternity. Instead of singing these beautiful psalms and hymns, you would be weeping and wailing and gnashing your teeth for ever in hell. Oh! may God, by His Spirit, tonight open your eyes to see your awful and imminent danger. There is nothing but the very skin on your ribs between your soul and hell. Just that heart-beat between you and hell. Do you know, dear friend, that there are scores in hell tonight who sat where you sit now, and hear what you hear now? They thought just as you think now. They never intended to be in hell. They made up their mind about that, must as you are making up yours now. They heard just such messages as you have been hearing. They said the same things you have said about them. Some of them even laughed at the thought of hell and made fun of the preacher who told them about it, just as you are doing now, but there they are in hell for eternity. How did they get there? Let us hear them speak. "How did you get there?" "I got here because I put off too long." "Did you intend to go there?" "Oh, no! I made up my mind that I would some day repent and believe, but I put it off too long." I fear some of you will be there, too, and with the very same wail on your lips, for you are doing the very best thing to grieve God and please the devil, and damn your own soul. You don't need to be a drunkard to be damned, or a blasphemer or harlot. Oh, no! All you need to do is to reject Christ - just what you are doing now - and as sure as the sun sets tonight and will rise tomorrow, in hell you will open your eyes, being in torment.

Oh, I beseech you, do not delay any longer. Why should you perish? God loved you and gave His Son to die for you. Trust Him now, for **now** is the accepted time, **now** is the day of salvation. Don't believe your own notions if they are contrary to God's Word, or the notions of others, however good and wise they seem to be, but take God's Word for it and flee from wrath.

FOUR QUESTIONS

There are four questions I will try to answer on this subject.

First, **What of the certainty of hell?**
Second, **What is the nature of hell?**
Third, **Where is hell?"**
Fourth, **How shall we escape hell?**

I. THE CERTAINTY OF HELL

Can we be really sure there is a hell? What authority have we for declaring there is such a place? There are so many opinions about it. Some very good and learned men deny the fact of it altogether. I can't think that a loving God would condemn a soul to hell for a short life of sin here. Isn't it strange, you rarely if ever, get unconverted men disbelieving in hell. They may say they don't believe when things are well with them, but when they come to face death, then they certainly believe. It is usually the converted man who discredits the truth about it, for it sort of eases his conscience for not doing anything to save lost souls. He has an excuse for his laziness and indifference regarding the perishing. He talks about the "Fatherhood of God" and the "Brotherhood of Man". If God is the Father of all, then hell is an impossibility and an insult to God and man. But God is not the Father of all. Is He the Father of the devil? No; He is the creator of the devil. You might as well talk about God being the Father of dogs and cats and trees, as say He is the Father of all men. It is not right to confound creatorship and fatherhood.

CONFUSION

I remember a very nice refined-looking lady came to me after she heard me preach on hell, and she said, "You are a father, and I am sure love your children." I said I did. She then said, "I suppose if you could ease the pain of sorrow of your child you would do so?" I said I would. She said, "What do you think of a father who could save his child from suffering and did not do so?" I said he would be a tyrant and a monster. She said, "I am glad to hear you say so, for, you see, that is what you are making God out to be. God could never see His children in hell and torment. He would be a monster if He did." "But," I said, "lady, you just make one mistake, and that is, God hasn't a child in hell and never will have one there. There are none on the road there, either. All God's children are either in heaven or on the road there, and dead sure of getting there. The people who are in hell are the devil's bairns. God as a Father has a home for His children, so the devil is a father, and he has a home for his children." If you have never been born again, you are of your father, the devil, and his works you do. God is only the Father of those who believe in Jesus Christ, and are His born again ones. I believe it is this damnable heresy in the churches today that is causing men to cease believing in hell. My friends, there is surely a hell, for the Bible clearly teaches it. No honest reader can come to the Word of God and shut his eyes to it. It is as clear and real as the teaching about heaven. It's strange how they all believe there is a heaven and yet they only know that there is such a place because the Bible teaches it, and yet they deny the teaching of the same Bible when it teaches about hell. Such a position is illogical and unreasonable. If there is no hell, then there is no infallible Bible, and we are left to the opinions of men and their speculations. If there is no hell, then we have no Christ or Christianity. The churches are just a farce, and the Sunday preaching just a waste of time. It is Christ and hell, or no hell, no Christ. Christ stands or falls with hell.

CHRIST OR HELL?

If this Bible is the Word of God - and it is - if Jesus Christ is the Son of God - and He is - then there is a hell. You may deny this fact, but that will not destroy it. Whether I believe a fact or not will never alter that fact. Fire burns, whether I believe it or not. Poison kills, whether I believe it or not. Frost freezes, whether I believe it or not. The sun rises and sets whether I believe it or not. The world is round, whether I believe it or not. Two and two make four, whether I believe it or not. Hell is a reality, whether I believe it or not. I'll be there if I reject Christ, whether I believe it or not.

"But," you say, "don't you know that learned men have changed the word 'hell'?" I know that. What right they have to do so, I don't know. But suppose they have changed the word or name, does that alter the fact or the nature of the place? Suppose I said there was no such country as this, or changed the name of this country, would that destroy the country or alter it any? You know right well it wouldn't. You may change my name, but you won't change me or obliterate me. I am just the same fellow with another name. You may call a vulture a bird of paradise, but it is just the same old scavenger. You may call a skunk a canary, but he won't sing on that account, neither will its smell be any sweeter. You may call hell by whatever name you care, but it is just the same awful place where they weep and wail and gnash their teeth. It sounds nice to call it "the grave," "Sheol," "Tartarus," "Gehenna". It sounds very scholarly and nice to the ear, but don't forget it is just the same fearful place of torment. You tell some man you are angry with to go to "Gehenna," and he'll think that you mean him to go for a holiday somewhere, or that you are wishing him well. But you tell him to go to hell, and he will soon let you know what he thinks of you. I fear there is a danger here. By changing words we may take away the fear and fact of such a place from men's minds.

NOT A PARABLE

But maybe there is someone here who says, "It isn't good exegesis to base a doctrine on a parable." The Scripture I read just now wasn't a parable. When our Lord used a parable He let us know that it was one, but this is not a parable, it is the relation of an actual fact that was known to those who heard Him tell it. "There was a certain rich man." "There was a certain beggar." He gives their names and their manner of life, and how they lived. I can imagine how those who listened would whisper to each other and say, "We knew Lazarus. Many a time we helped him." "We know the rich man He is talking about, and many a time passed his home." So He did not invent the story to enforce the truth, but He took a local incident, and by it He burned in this truth. The rich man did not go to hell because he was rich. There is no vice in riches, there is no virtue in poverty. He went to hell because he left God out of his life. The poor man went to heaven because he trusted in the Lord. It is always that way.

We are also sure there is a hell, because common sense demands one. I can never understand the minds of those who will not allow God to have a hell for men and women who will not have His Son to be their Saviour. Yet in these civilised lands of ours we have large penitentiaries and gaols. What a shame it is to put men and women in such places of torment, and keep them there shut up from the world, robbing them of their liberties and privileges, and treating them like cattle or slaves. Separating men from their homes and families, and bringing pain and shame on their friends. Isn't it a shame that this civilisation should do such a thing? Many a time men are in gaol because they have done only one crime, and then some of them we take out and hang or electrocute. But you say, "Don't you know these people are law-breakers? It is for their own good and the safety of the country and the people that we put them in there and do this with them." You would look with pity on me if I talked like this about our gaols, and wonder what sort of mind I had, or where I came from.

COMMON SENSE

Do you think that we have more sense than God? Who are the people who go to hell? They are men and women who rebelled against God and refused to be saved by the blood of His Son. What else can God do with them but put them in prison? What sort of a world would it be if all the criminals were allowed to go free and do whatever they cared? Our person or our property would not be safe, and life would not be worth living. We have great big asylums all over the land. Thousands of people - good, nice and decent people at that - are kept there against their will; are taken from their homes against their will and shut up there. The treatment they get is not very comfortable at times. Isn't it a shame to have such places and treat people like that, seeing it is through no fault of theirs? I can imagine the look you would give me, and how you would wonder where I had come from. What contempt there would be in your voice when you would tell me. "Don't you know that these people are insane? They are not responsible. For their own sake and the safety of society they are put in such places." I see, I understand. But let me ask you, "Has God not got such a place for mad people, too, in eternity?" Certainly He has. Surely a man is mad who damns his own soul by wilfully rejecting Jesus Christ as his Saviour, in spite of the love of God and work of the Holy Spirit. What sort of a world would eternity be if all the people who would not have God to be their God (or His law to guide them, or rejected His Son as their Saviour) were allowed to go where they pleased and do as they pleased? Oh, no! men and women, hell is God's penitentiary; hell is God's madhouse. If you continue to rebel against God, God has a gaol for you, and if you are so foolish as to refuse His salvation, God has an asylum for you. God has just about as much common sense about such things as we have here on earth. God never sends a man to hell. Man goes there by the deliberate choice of his own will. You hear it said, "How could God be a God of love and send me there?"

A GOD OF LOVE

God never sent any man to hell. But such a statement as that suggests or implies the thought that they would not do such a thing as that - almost saying that they have more love and compassion for men than God has. I was conducting a campaign in West Australia one time. One day I received a letter from a preacher saying that if I would be more like Jesus I would preach more about heaven and less about hell. This made me go to my Bible and find out whether I was unlike Jesus preaching about hell so much. This is what I found. Jesus spoke about hell thirteen times, and in awful and gruesome language, and He only spoke about heaven once, "In my Father's house are many mansions." You would think by the way some people talk that they have more love for their fellow-men than Jesus has. Jesus is incarnate love. He so loved that He gave Himself for the salvation of men. Do you ever find these men who talk about loving their fellow-men ever dying or ever suffering to save them? Oh, no. They sit calmly by their firesides cooing like a turtle dove about love, while all the time they don't know the first thing about love. The one next to Jesus who told more about hell was John, the Apostle of love. As you read the Book of Revelation about hell, how terribly graphic and gruesome the description is. Do you mean to tell me that these turtle doves of today have more love, or know more abut love, than Jesus or John did? Surely not. But is it a mark of love for men to hide the truth from them because it is awful?

EXCURSION TRAIN

Suppose you had an excursion from this town. You were all in the train going to your destination. I was on the railway, and as I walked I came to a bridge and found it was broken. I knew your train with its hundreds on board was about due; in fact, I could hear it coming. I think for a moment. I will warn them of their danger and stop them. But then again I think, it would be a pity to spoil their holiday or any part of it. I might get people scared, and maybe some of them might faint. I love them so much and want them to have as nice a time as they can get, so I wave you Godspeed and wish you a good trip, while all the time I knew that right ahead of you was the broken bridge. The train rushed on and all on board were killed or mangled. The whole town is deluged in sorrow. I come down amongst you and tell you that I knew the bridge was down, but I loved the people so much I couldn't find it in my heart to warn them and spoil their fun, even for a few minutes. Tell me, how many of you would believe that love prompted such an action on my part? How long would they let me live in that town, or even live at all? What are we to say of men and ministers who stand before their fellows who are rushing to eternity as fast as time can take them, and to hell if they are without Christ, and yet never warn them of their imminent danger, or hide the fact of their danger from them by telling them that there is no hell? God is love, etc. The horror of it. The damnableness of it. Could you imagine a meaner thing than a man putting a man on the wrong road when he asked the way? I have had that done to me and it cost me hours and miles. It was a dirty, contemptible trick to play on any man. But that was only putting a man wrong in time. But to deliberately put men wrong for eternity without the hope of ever getting right, surely such a man is a Judas Iscariot, or worse. Just as sure as there is a heaven, there is a hell. The authority we have for the one is the same as the other. They both stand or fall together. If there is no hell, then there is no heaven.

II. THE NATURE OF HELL

All we know about the nature of this place we find in the Word of God. It is the same about heaven. All its glories and bliss are revealed in the Bible. We dare not take the notions of men about so serious a matter. We cannot describe fully the one or the other, but there are some things clearly revealed in His Word. Let us consider them.

DEATH

Hell is a place of death; no annihilation or cessation of life, but as life separated from God. There they never cease to live, they are dying but never die. On earth, death is the terror of kings and the king of terrors, but if death were to go to hell and it was known to the inmates there that they would cease to be, there would be joy in that dark, joyless world, for the agony of that place is their undying existence. "The worm dieth not and the fire is not quenched."

UNSATISFIED DESIRES

It is the place of unsatisfied desires. You created desires here and you tried to satisfy them, and in some measure you succeeded. But in hell you will be consumed with undying desire, eternally intensified, but eternally unsatisfied. Men here will murder for money, will endure hard work and little food for alcohol, will waste their bodies with toil and pain for pleasure. In hell they will still have the desire, but no means to gratify it. For ever and ever tormented with the cravings of the body they indulged here on earth. They will as surely have a body as the saints will. This man in hell wanted water. He felt the agony of the flames. He had eyes and a tongue. I pray you, do not get it into your heads that this is all metaphorical. What sort of punishment would it be if a judge sentenced a man to be hung, but only metaphorically? It would be ridiculous, and it is just as ridiculous to think that in hell they are only spirits.

VILE COMPANIONSHIP

It is a place of vile companionship. The vilest and the worst that ever have been on the earth. The scum of creation will be there. What a hell it will be for some who have been reared in refinement and culture, loving everything lovely and of good report, but still rejecting Christ, to be cast into hell with liars and adulterers and murderers and fornicators and all abominable creatures. To have to live amongst such here - you would rather be dead. You will have to live with such for ever and ever and never be able to die or remove to some other place. Oh! I pray you, who are so loving and lovable and lovely in your life, why should you perish and dwell in such a place for ever? Turn ye, why will ye die?

NO HOPE

It is a place without hope. The reason you can now sit and listen to all this with not a tremor or a fear, is because you hope that it is not true or that you will never be there, but some way, some time, you will repent and believe. It is only a false hope, for you have no right to presume on the mercy and love of God. You may want to come when you wish, but you may not be able. The Lord says to such, "When you call I will not answer." You are so buoyed and built up with a false hope that you imagine that you can make a convenience of God, that He must be at your beck and call when you want Him and where, but you have not one single promise to build such hope upon. There will be no hope in hell to thus buoy you up. It is a place of hopeless despair. Hope has never entered its portals and never will. You leave all hope behind you when you come to die, if you are without Christ. Hopeless gloom and darkness reign there forever.

RUIN

It is a place of increasing ruin. I remember one time saying that if I were to get to hell and be allowed to preach to the lost souls there, that I would not have to plead with them as I have to do here. An old retired preacher came to me afterwards and said, that if I were allowed to preach in hell, that I would not be able to get one of them to repent, for if they were not saved here by the mercy and love of God they would never be saved by the fire and the pain of hell. It is true. The ruin begins here and goes on and on for ever. You will be far worse in hell than here, and through all eternity will be getting further and further into ruin. That is why it is called the "bottomless" pit. It has no bottom. It is awful to even think of. Will you not be warned to flee from such awful and irretrievable ruin?

MEMORY

It is also a place of memory. I am not very concerned whether you believe that there is literal fire in hell. It seems to me that if there was, it would ease the anguish and the agony of those who are there. But you will have memory. It will be awakened never to sleep again. Here you are able to drug it with the drink or the dance or the lust of gold. You are able to forget here, but you will never be able to forget there. The agony of it! When men are haunted by an awakening memory here, they commit suicide. You will not be able to do that there. You must live. You must remember. Memory will be like ten thousand mirrors around you reflecting and recalling the sins and follies of this life. You will there remember the greatness of the glory you lost. It is a very light thing to you now. You would sell it for a night's pleasure in sin, a few acres of land, or a few pieces of gold, but then you will be able to form some adequate idea of its worth. You will remember you could have obtained it. That will be hell in itself. It will be indescribable agony to know that you might have been walking the streets of gold and singing the new song, and filled with the felicities and the bliss of the saved, but now by your own folly and will you are condemned to eternal darkness and despair and torment. You will remember the many lost opportunities you had. You laughed when you had the chance to repent and believe. You said lightly that you had plenty of time. Oh, the anguish of remembering!

You must think abut it. Things will pass and repass before your mind to your eternal torment. You will remember how often you were urged to flee from the wrath to come. You thought your mother was a scare-monger when she so often desired you to repent. She wearied you with her continual pleadings. You laughed at the preacher when he tried to alarm you. The sermon was long and a weariness to you. You slept under his preaching. You scorned the friend who tried to get you to trust the Lord Jesus. All their pleadings are past forever and you are left with the pain and remorse of memory as you think of all this. Your mother's tears will scald you then. The voice of entreaty will haunt you through all eternity.

SOLD CHEAP

You will remember the easy terms on which you might have received eternal life and escaped death. This will be the sorest of all. If it had been impossible for you to repent, or if you had no choice in the matter, or if your circumstances were such that you could not believe, it would make the agony easier; but to know that you might have had a life of eternal bliss with the purified for the accepting, will burn you with an unquenchable fire and torment you as an undying worm. You will remember what you sold your soul for. Some of you are selling your soul for liquor, some for fame, some for gold. If only you had the satisfaction of knowing that you made a good bargain for your soul it might ease the torments there, but oh, the agony when you remember how cheaply you sold eternal bliss and bought an eternity of woe and agony. You will remember you wilfully did it. Here you blame the Christians for their hypocrisy. You blame everyone, even God, but there you will find out that you are the guilty one, and that deliberately and wilfully you sealed your doom and secured your damnation. For all eternity you will be blaming yourself and tormenting yourself for your folly and pride.

You will remember how hard you wrought to get to hell. "The way of the transgressor is hard." How true this is! It speaks as loudly as Calvary speaks of the love of God. If God had not been love he might have made the way to hell easy and fast, but He has hedged the way there with thorns and barriers, and a man must work hard to get there. He has to stifle conscience again and again. He has to tramp over the tears and the prayers of God's people. He has to silence God's Word, quench the Holy Spirit, trample underfoot the precious blood of Christ; all this before he goes there and succeeds in damning his soul for ever. If God does not love us we would have been in hell long ago, but He would not let us go even when we were wed to our sin and determined on our eternal destruction.

Surely I have said enough about the nature of hell, but before I leave this part of my subject, let me give you some more of the terms used by God to depict the nature of this place. Some people would give you the idea that there was very little in the Bible about hell, and what preachers said about it was taken from some isolated portion of it and was greatly exaggerated by their preaching. Here are some of the terms used by the Lord, and after you have read them I am sure you won't think lightly of the place, or think that it is some picnic or half-way house on the road to heaven.

THE BIBLE HELL

"A lake of fire," "A bottomless pit," "A horrible tempest," "A devouring fire," "A place of sorrows," "Where they wail," "A place of weeping," "A furnace," "A place of torments," "Everlasting burnings," "A place of filthiness," "Where they curse God," "Everlasting destruction," "A place of outer darkness," "Where they have no rest," "Where they pray," "Where they never repent," "Everlasting punishment," "Where they gnaw their tongues," "Blackness and darkness for ever," "Prepared for the devil and his angels," "Where they cry for a drop of water," "Their breath is a living flame," "They are tormented with fire and brimstone," "There are dogs, sorcerers, whoremongers, murderers and un-believers," "They drink the wine of the wrath of God," "They don't want their friends to come," "Their worm dieth not and the fire is not quenched," "Hell fire," "Hell" "Second death," "Chains of darkness," "Wrath to come." These are only some of the many terms used in the Word of God to describe this place, and I am sure they are not idle words, or words carelessly used, but the sober truth of God. To me it is awful, and yet I fear some of you are tired of hearing about it and treating it all as if it were a myth. I beseech you treat not this message in that way, but believe it and repent ere it is too late. You may be saying that I have overdrawn the statements, but, friend, if ever you get there, you will then say that the half was never told. Take no risks, be saved from sin now, and hell hereafter.

III. WHERE IS HELL?

Hell begins where man's day of grace ends here. There are so many who imagine they can be saved when and where they like. That just when they take the notion they can flee from the wrath to come and escape hell. This is the devil's delusion to damn your soul. The Word says: "Seek ye the Lord while He may be found." "Call ye upon Him while He is near." You may seek Him and not find Him. You may call when He is not near. Jesus told the men of His day, "Ye shall seek Me and shall not find Me; and where I am, thither ye cannot come."

"There is a time, we know not when,
A place, we know not where,
That seals the destiny of men
for glory or despair."

You may reject Christ for the last time now, then your day of grace has come and gone for ever. That is where hell begins for you and every other soul who has sinned their day of grace away. God is under no obligation to accept you. Salvation is of purest grace. It is of the Lord. You never will deserve it or be able to buy it or merit it. If you are to be saved you must accept it as a poor undeserving and hell-deserving sinner. Be warned, unsaved one, and if you have the least inclination to be saved don't kill it by putting off accepting Christ any longer. But just now, where you are and as you are, trust Him with your soul and be saved for eternity. This is God's day of grace. Tomorrow it may have passed for you, and you may live a good, decent, happy, religious life for forty years after, and in that living body of yours may dwell a doomed, dead and damned soul. You say, where is hell? Listen and I'll put it in a sentence. Hell is the end of every Christ-rejecting life - every Christless life. You may belong to the church and be very devoted in your attendance on the means of grace. You may give your body to be burned; you may preach with the eloquence of men and angels, and have all faith so that you could move mountains, you may have all knowledge and wisdom, but if you have not Christ, that moment you close your eyes in time you will open them in hell, being in torment. The moment a born-again one dies they are in the conscious presence of the Lord. As soon as a Christless man dies he is in hell and conscious torment. This is not a fable cunningly devised to scare you, but it is the truth of God. It would be better and safer for you to trust the Word of God and not depend on the notions of men, however learned or great they may be. There is a way that seemeth right unto a man, but the end is death. You may reject the truth of God and accept your own opinions or the opinions of others, and have perfect satisfaction and peace by so doing, but the end of death is hell just the same, although they may give you a Christian burial and say many nice things about you, that will not make your torment any easier, or your condition any cooler. Be wise and be warned in time to seek the Lord while He may be found. Accept Him as your Saviour and Lord and you will never perish, but have everlasting life.

IV. HOW ARE WE TO ESCAPE HELL?

This the part of my message that I like. The other part has been very hard to declare to you, but to be true to your soul I had to do it. I will never regret doing it, if you have been led to flee from the wrath to come. It will not be any joy to me to know you are damned, but, oh, it would be added joy and glory to know that you have decided to believe in Christ. None need perish. You may have raked in the very kennels of hell, your sins may be as black as the pit and as numerous as the sand on the seashore; the fires of hell would be a ripe and rich harvest for the seeds of iniquity you have sown; still there is mercy with the Lord here and now. Jesus Christ has died, the just for you, the unjust. He was bruised for your iniquities. He was wounded for your transgressions. Surely you will not go to hell with your eyes open and your feet stained with the blood of Christ.

O, *be saved, His grace is free,*
O, *be saved, He died for thee.*

In the north of Scotland, where the main line crosses a great ravine or gully - a fearful looking abyss - the viaduct that bridged it was one of the wonders of the North. One night a fearful storm raged over the district. The little stream or burn that meandered under the viaduct was turned into a raging mad torrent. A young highland shepherd laddie sheltered his sheep as best he could for the night. In the morning, long before dawn, he set out to see how they had fared. As he made his way up the hillside he noticed to his horror that the central column had gone and that the bridge was broken. He knew that the mail train was due, and that if not warned she would be dashed to pieces and many lives lost. He looked at the raging torrent. He wondered if he could get across. The thought of the danger of so many urged him on. He plunged in, and made his way to the other side. He was battered and baffled and breathless and bleeding when he got to the other side. He made his way up as best he could, wondering if he would be in time. As soon as he reached the rails he heard the "pound, pound" of the mighty engine. He stood and beckoned wildly, but all he saw was the hand of the engineer beckoning him out of the way. He was making up lost time. The train came on nearer and nearer, and still he stood beckoning it to stop. At last it came to where he was. He flung himself in front of the engine. The driver put on the brakes suddenly and managed to stop the train almost in its own length. The stop was so sudden that the passengers were awakened, and came out to see what was the matter. When they could see nothing they were very angry, but the driver said, "It has been a close shave this time. We might all have been lost." And when they saw how near they were to the ragged edge of the broken bridge, their faces blanched. The driver said, "Come with me and I will show you the one who saved us tonight." They went with him back along the track a little way, and there they saw the mangled remains of the young highland shepherd laddie. "If he had not died for us," said the engine driver "we would all have perished tonight."

That is what the Lord Jesus did for us on the cross. He flung Himself between us and the wrath of hell. He died for us, or we would have died. What base ingratitude it would have been on the part of the passengers in that train if they had not felt grateful for what that lad had done for them, but what base ingratitude on your part to spurn Christ's love and make light of His death on the cross. Tell me, will you rush over His body to hell? Why should you perish? There is no need. God loves you and desires your salvation. Jesus died to save you from sin and hell. Accept Him. Trust Him. Believe Him, and you shall never perish. But if you spurn His love and mercy, you will surely perish. May God incline your hearts to come to Him now.

Heaven

---- ❖ ----

"Eye hath not seen, nor ear heard, neither have entered into the heart of man, the things which God hath prepared for them that love Him" I Corinthians 2: 9

There is no subject that inflames the heart and fires the imagination more than the subject of heaven. After being away from home and loved ones for a long time, the very thought of going home again fills the heart with joy. Should it not be the same when we think of our heavenly home?

There are three reasons why every Christian should delight in this theme.

FIRST, WE ARE SURELY GOING THERE

"None perish that trust Him". When we are thinking of visiting any other country or city, we like to find out all we can about it, so that when we get there we will know what is most interesting and where to look for it, and thus get the most and best out of our visit. Shall we do other about heaven? When the Lord Jesus has taken the trouble to go and prepare a place for us and has given us much information about the place, should we not take time to find out all we can about it, so that when we get there we will not feel as if we were strangers or foreigners. We will feel at home. There are many Christians who know more about the Continent of Europe or Great Britain or America than they do about heaven. This should not be.

SECOND, WE ARE GOING 'HOME'

It is to be the bride's home. That is why the Lord Jesus - the Bridegroom - is away from us now. He said, "I go to prepare a place for you, and if I go and prepare a place for you I will come again, and receive you unto myself; that where I am there ye may be also." Since He has told us this, surely it would be a slight to Him if we were unconcerned about the place or the preparations. The joy of any bridegroom when he is making ready the home for his bride, is her joyful interest in all that is being done for her. If she were indifferent or uninterested in all that was being done for her, it would be very sore on the bridegroom and a slight on his love. So when we are showing any interest in this theme we are showing in some measure our appreciation of all He is preparing for us and we are rejoicing His heart in the doing of it.

THIRD, SADNESS WILL BE CHANGED TO GLADNESS

Meditation upon this theme will change monotony and drudgery into glory and gladness. Are we in sorrow? Some loved one has left us for the better land? Surely the thought that they are only on the other side, and that soon we too will be with them, to meet to part no more, should bring us great comfort in our sorrow. Are we weary and tired with life's battles and struggles? Isn't it grand to know that soon we will be where there will never be another fight or struggle, and where we can never be weary again? What strength it gives us to go on and never give in! Then when we think that we may be there any moment! "In a moment, in the twinkling of an eye!" Hallelujah. The last sorrow or pain felt! The last burden or care carried! The last struggle ended! The last fight past! Done for ever with the drudgery of our common lives! The last floor washed, the last garment mended, the last meal cooked! The common round and daily toil ended for ever! Surely such a hope as that gladdens and lightens our hearts and nerves us on to fresh endeavours.

HALF NEVER TOLD

However long we may meditate on this theme or however diligently, we will never be able to exhaust it. "Eye hath not seen, ear hath not heard." I remember reading of a child born blind. He had never seen the beauties or the glories of nature. His loved ones had done their best to make him see by describing them to him; but however well we may describe these things we can never tell them as they really are. So it was with him. They heard about some clever oculist who had performed some very remarkable operations and they took the lad to him. He examined him very carefully and then he said that he thought the operation would give the boy his sight, but they were not to be too sure; he would do his best, and if he did not succeed the boy would be none the worse afterwards and they would have the satisfaction of knowing that all possible had been done for the lad. The operation was performed. The lad was to keep the bandages on for some days after. At last the day came to take them off, and then it would be known if the operation had been successful. The excitement was intense. The mother and father and some friends were there. The room was darkened. The bandages were removed. The light was admitted very slowly at first, and then fully. What joy there was when they saw that the lad had his sight. He was taken over to the window of the ward and shown the glories of the early spring. He was silent, and they wondered what was wrong. They looked into his face and saw tears running down his cheeks. In answer to their questionings, he said, "Why did you not tell me what a lovely place I was living in?" They had done their best, but they had failed to give him any adequate conception of the beauties of nature. So it will be when we get to heaven. We will say, "The half was never told." Who could adequately describe the glories and felicities of the home above, where all is love? There is one thing true and that is, that all that is best and most precious here is plentiful there. The hearts of all are filled with love. The songs are all glad, and the streets are gold. How rare such things are here! Still there is much in God's Word that can thrill and cheer our hearts. Let us consider some of the things told us about heaven.

HEAVEN IS A PLACE

The Bible describes heaven as a place. John 14: 2 says, "In My Father's house are many mansions; if it were not so I would have told you; I go to prepare a place for you." It is not a *state*, but a *place*. As real a place as any place we know of on this earth. Where it is we cannot tell, but the Bible always speaks of it as being up. It is somewhere other than this world, but it is really a place and we can tell from the Word of God what the place is like.

IT IS A PLACE OF BRIGHTNESS

We know that it is bright there, not so much by the things that are mentioned that will be there, but by the things mentioned that won't be there. There will be no NIGHT there. It is one long eternal day. The sun never sets. The Lord is the Light of Heaven. I don't know how you feel about it, but to me this fact fills me with joy. I cannot say I am afraid of the night, but I am never comfortable or happy in the dark. We always associate every evil and horrible thing with the night. Storms and sickness usually begin and break out at night. Homes are robbed and murders committed at night. So it is only natural that we don't like the night. When we get to heaven we will never have this dread, for there will be no night there.

There will be no DEATH in heaven. They never die or grow old. No funeral has ever darkened its streets. There are no cemeteries there. A dying woman said to her brother, who was about to take his leave of her without any hope of meeting her again in this world. "Brother, I trust we shall meet in the land of the living. We are now in the land of the dying." How true it is. How different things will be there from this world, for we cannot get away from the fact of death here. We may not believe very much, we may deny everything but there is one thing we must believe in and cannot deny, and that is death. Glory to God! That spectre will never darken the brightness of that land of life.

Again, the brightness has never been dimmed by SORROW. The world is full of it now. It is impossible to find a home here where sorrow has not entered. Every life has its share of it. As you look over a crowd of people, it is striking to notice how many there are who are dressed in black, mourning the loss of some loved one or ones. They are dressed in garments of white up there. There are many shining faces down here, but behind a shining face there is many a heart filled with sorrow. What an infinite variety there is of sorrow. The most of it never seen or known.

PAIN is unknown there. None escape it here; it is the common lot of all. Many would be glad to die that they might be free from what is almost unbearable - having hardly known an hour for years that they have not been racked with pain. Many have a pain at the heart far sorer than any physical pain. A child gone astray in sin. Can anyone fathom the pain such a mother endures? Thank God! there will be none of that there.

Then it is so bright there; no eye will be dimmed by TEARS. 'This world is full of sighs, full of sad and weeping eyes.' A tear has never dimmed the eye there. I don't know what you women will do when you get there, for tears are your friends in many a time of trouble. Frequently I have heard a women say that many a time she went away and had a good cry to herself. Her tears acted like a sort of safety valve for her. Then what a weapon it is in the hands of women. Just start them flowing, and what man or argument could stand before them? The Lord will see that up there there will be no occasion for them, so they won't be needed. Glory to God! not only unclouded skies, but undimmed eyes for all who gather there.

Finally, there will be no CURSE there. How many are cursed by sin here - the sin of parents or friends. Twisted limbs, weak minds, ruined constitutions. Oh! the amount of curse there is here. Thank God! we are going to a world where the curse and blight of sin is forever done away with. These things will give us some idea of the brightness of that world.

HAPPINESS FO N THERE

It is also a place of HAPPINESS. There is nothing gloomy or sad in that land. We read of choirs singing and the redeemed singing their blood-passion song. "Unto Him who loved us and loosed us from our sins in His own blood." One of the Minor Prophets, with prophetic vision tells us that the streets are full of children playing not crying. What happiness children bring to the home, and it seems to me that is one of the reasons why so many die in childhood; the Lord would have heaven as bright and happy as He can make it. They never know envy or jealousy or hatred or malice or wars there. These are the things that curse our lives and land here. We shall dwell in the happiness of eternal and perfect love. Some places here are sour, and some people too, but nothing of the kind is known there. Dr. Guthrie, of Edinburgh, says, "Heaven is greatly made up of little children - sweet buds that have never blown, or that death has plucked from a mother's bosom to lay on his own cold breast, just when they were expanding, flower-like and opening their engaging beauties in the budding time and the springtime of life. 'Of such is the Kingdom of Heaven.' How soothing these words are by the cradle of a dying infant! They fall like balm-drops on our bleeding hearts, when we watch the ebbing of that young life, as wave after wave breaks feebler and the sinking breath gets lower and lower, till with a gentle sigh and a passing quiver of the lip, our sweet child leaves its body like an angel asleep and ascends to the beatitudes of heaven and the bosom of its God. Perhaps God does with His heavenly garden as we do with our own. He chiefly takes it from nurseries, and select for transplanting what is yet in its young and tender age - flowers before they have bloomed and trees ere they begin to bear."

CONSCIOUSNESS

It is also a place of CONSCIOUSNESS. So many are perplexed and wonder whether they will know the loved ones who have gone before. The Word of God is very clear about this. We read, "For now we see through a glass darkly; but then face to face." What sort of place would it be if we did not recognise each other? Here we know each other very imperfectly. Shall we know each other less there? Nay; we shall know each other better when the mists have rolled away. Peter recognised Moses and Elijah on the Mount of Transfiguration. They were not changed, and that is why he recognised them. How often, when someone is entering death, they have seen some one loved long since but lost a while! When good Queen Victoria was dying she was heard to say, "Albert! Albert!" Her husband who had died years before, was near her. I knew a lady who told me that when her little child was passing way, she seemed to wake up and her face light up, and she cried, "Papa, papa." The father had gone before some time. Are we not to believe all this evidence? What makes any place dear to us? Is it not the presence of loved ones there? If we will not know each other we will not know the Lord Jesus. No, no, that could never be. The recognition of the one who ensures the recognition of the other. Surely there shall no knowledge cease which now we have, but only that which implies our imperfection. And what imperfection can this imply? Nay, our present knowledge shall be increased beyond belief. It shall indeed be done away, but as the light of the candle, or the light of the stars is done away by the rising sun; so it is more a doing away of our ignorance than of our knowledge. I must confess, as the experience of my soul, that the expectation of loving my friends in heaven kindles my love to them on earth. If I thought I should never know them, and consequently never love them after this life is ended, I should, in reason number them with temporal things, and love them as such; but I now delightfully converse with my pious friends, in a firm persuasion that I shall converse with them forever; and I take comfort in those of them who are dead or absent, as believing I shall shortly meet them in heaven, and love them with a love which shall be perfected.

However much we may long to see the loved ones, we will want far more to see the ONE who saved us and loved us with a dying and undying love. "HIM whom having not seen, we love." When the little boy who was operated on successfully, saw, the first thing he asked for was, that he might see the one who had given him his sight. It will be the same with us when we get there. It is not a sleep after death, for to be absent from the body is to be present with the Lord and loved ones. When we die we shall awake in His likeness. We will then know everything perfectly. The problems and the perplexities here will all be solved. The knowledge that we longed for here will be ours there. No more mysteries nor uncertainties. We shall know perfectly.

HEAVEN, A KINGDOM

Then heaven is not only a place, but it is a kingdom. It is as real as any earthly kingdom, but what a difference from the kingdoms of this world. Here we have rulers and kings, but at the best they are only sinners with crowns on their heads. It is necessary for them to be guarded everywhere they go, and they have to maintain large armies and navies or they would be dethroned. But in that kingdom there will be nothing but perfect love between subject and sovereign and among all the people. Neither wars nor rumours of wars are known there. Everyone will have perfect sight. None will be crippled or deformed or stunted. Our knowledge will be perfected, the mists will have for ever passed away.

HEAVEN, A CITY

Heaven is also a city. What a city that will be! No slums or saloons there. No hospitals or jails. No poor or depressed ones. The very things that curse our great cities here will be absent. The city which God hath prepared is as imperishable in its inhabitants as its materials. Its pearl, its jasper, its pure gold are only immortal to frame the abode of immortals. No cry of death is in any of its dwellings. No funerals darken any of its ways. No sepulchre of the holiest relics gleam among the everlasting hills. Its streets are pure gold. Its homes are mansions, its inhabitants are holy and happy. A city that never was built with hands, nor hoary with the years of time; a city whose inhabitants no census has numbered; a city through whose streets no tides of business runs; a city without griefs or graves, without sins or sorrows, without births or burials, without marriage or mournings; a city which glories in having Jesus for its King, angels for its guards, saints for its citizens; whose walls are salvation and whose gates are praise.

HEAVEN, OUR HOME

Heaven is to be our home. This view appeals to us most. It is impossible to define home, but we all know what it means. Home, oh, how sweet is that word! What beautiful and tender associations cluster thick around it! Compared with it, house, mansion, palace, are cold, heartless terms. But home! that word quickens the pulse, warms the heart, stirs the soul to its depths, makes age feel young again, rouses apathy into energy, sustains and inspires and imparts patient endurance. We delight to think of it. A friend bending over a dying saint was expressing his sorrow to see him so low. With the radiant countenance rather of one who has just left heaven than one about to enter it, he raised and clasped his hands and exclaimed in ecstasy, "I am going home."

I can imagine some mother here, whose life has been all toil and labour, say to herself that the thought of heaven being a home does not appeal to her much, for home to her here, while having many joys, has had much toil and weariness. It is the mother who is last to bed and the first to rise. When any are sick she is there day and night. She is always planning and arranging for others. The thought of a home is not altogether pleasant to her, but God's home is a home of rest. There are no tired limbs or weary minds in it. I remember a mother leaving her family and going to a sanatorium for a rest; after she had been there for some time, she wrote home to the loved ones an said that she felt as if she were in heaven. She had nothing to do or to bother about; all was done for her. Do you mean to tell me that men can make a place where weary and tired mothers can have a rest and God not do better? That could never be. As the body when it is buried in the grave rests there, free from the fear of disease and death; free from assault and war; resting as in an impregnable fortress, dreading no hunger or thirst or alarms or death or disease; so the soul when it enters through the portals of the Home above, rests from its labours, cares, anxieties, temptations, enemies, rests in the peace, purity, joy, happiness, protection and endless benedictions of God.

HEAVEN, AN INHERITANCE

Heaven is also an inheritance. It is incorruptible and undefiled, and never passes away. How many there are who are selling such an inheritance for a few corruptible acres of land here which they cannot take away with them. Our inheritance is ours sure, for it is being reserved in heaven for us who are kept by the power of God through faith. There is no fear of our being done out of it by either friend or foe. It will be worthy of our heavenly Father's wealth.

NO SEA THERE

I have been trying to show you some of the glories of that land that is fairer than day, but there is one thing that is mentioned that will not be there, that I, for one, will sadly miss. It is this, "There will be no more sea." I have lived by the sea all my life. I have sailed on it for years. I love its roar and roll. Its noise is music.

Three-fourths of this world is sea. What a want there will be there! But we must not take these words literally but symbolically. What is the sea the symbol of? What does it suggest to our minds?

There are four things at least that the sea speaks to us about.

STORMS

The sea suggests storms. What a stormy life John had lived! He was an old man and lived for the testimony of Christ. What storms he had passed through - storms of persecution. Again and again he had been baffled and beaten by them and now he is wearied and tired, and as he sat there on that rock-bound Isle of Patmos that Lord's day he was in the spirit and he began to think of the home over there. The Lord gave him a look in, and the very thing that was shrieking and roaring in his ears then was not to be seen there. There were no more storms. Are not our lives like that too? It does not matter how quietly we may have lived, we have had our storms to encounter. If we are truly His and living out and out for Him, we will surely suffer persecution. The world has not changed in its attitude to the Lord, and because we bear His name, the world will give us a very stormy time.

Praise God! when we leave this realm we will have no more storms. We have had storms of temptation and trial and sorrow, again and again, until we have thought at times that our frail barque would be o'erwhelmed. Let us remember that we have the Lord of sea and sky with us, and we can never be lost with Him on board. What cyclones of passion we have come through; we have been almost sucked into their fatal centre! Sun and star at times seemed to have ceased to shine, so dark was the night. We have weathered them all and will until we reach the other shore where the storms of life will be o'er. Every storm is a fair wind to the child of God, for He is working all things together for our good. They but blow us on our way home.

RESTLESSNESS

The sea also speaks to us of restlessness. You never saw the sea perfectly still. It is always in motion. It has a twofold motion, it fluctuates and undulates. It rises and falls and goes to and fro. Isn't that like our lives? What restless creatures we are. We are never satisfied here and never will be until we awake in His likeness. We are always consumed with restless longings and yearnings. Aims and ambitions come and go. Today, we are up on the hill of hope, joy and faith; tomorrow, we are down in the valley of the shadow of death. Like Noah's dove, we can find no rest on the troubled waters of this life; but we are making for the haven of rest, where we shall forever be at rest and satisfied.

SEPARATION

The sea speaks to us of separation. How quickly the family is scattered! We are separated by the sea. How easily we might meet each other, but there is the great sea, with its dread and danger. There will be no separation there; we will meet to part no more. We also live very lonely and separated lives. We talk about companionships in life, and they certainly are very sweet. There is immeasurable helpfulness in strong, true friendships. Still it is true that however many, faithful and sympathetic our friends may be, we must enter and pass through life's crises alone. Everyone of us really lives a solitary life. We do not fight in companies and battalions and regiments, but as individuals. Each one must live his own life. "Everyone must bear his own burden." We are mysteries to each other. It is because we do not understand each other that we offend or are offended. It becomes irksome to us at times, and the sense of our solitude is almost unbearable. It is grand to know that we are making for a country where there is no separation. How truly the poet has written:

> "Not understood, we move along asunder,
> Our paths grow wider as the seasons creep
> Along the years; we marvel and we wonder
> Why life is life; and then we fall asleep
> Not Understood.

Not understood. We gather false impressions,
And hug them closer as the years go by,
Till virtues almost seem to us transgressions;
And thus men rise and fall, and live and die
Not Understood.

Not understood. Poor souls with stunted vision,
Oft measured giants by their narrow gauge;
The poisoned shafts of falsehood and derision
Are oft impelled 'gainst those who mould the age -
Not Understood.

Not understood. The secret springs of action,
Which lie beneath the surface and the show,
Are disregarded; with self satisfaction
We judge our neighbours, and they often go -
Not Understood.

Not understood. How trifles often change us -
The thoughtless sentence or the fancied slight
Destroy long years of friendship, and estrange us,
And on our souls their falls a freezing blight -
Not Understood.

Not understood. How many breasts are aching
For lack of sympathy! Ah, day by day
How many cheerless hearts are breaking!
How many noble spirits pass away
Not Understood.

O God! that men would see a little clearer,
Or judge less harshly where they cannot see;
O God! that men would draw a little nearer
To one another: they'd be nearer Thee
And Understood."

The gulf that is fixed between us here will then be gone forever and we shall know each other perfectly and love all the same.

Then we have many who have crossed the Bar before us and entered into their rest and home. They have left us here mourning the loss. The chair is vacant. The voice is silent. They are separated from us by the sea of death. How hopeless we would be and how little comfort we would have if we had no hope of a reunion again. It is this hope that helps to dry our tears and makes us strong to bear the separation. A missionary out in India had two little children - a boy and a girl. The little girl of three took ill and passed away in a few days; then the little boy took ill also. They saw that it was diphtheria. They were many miles away from the doctor. They heard that one had come to a village some miles away from them. They took but the little fellow and journeyed many miles through the jungles to the village only to find when they got there that he had gone. All they could do was watch the little life flicker away. Then they journeyed back again to their station, and laid the two wee darlings in the one grave. The mother said that she never seemed to feel the sorrow until all was over; then when she came into the home and put away for the last time their toys and garments, it was too much for her. She collapsed. She lay for some days ill; but, speaking about it afterwards, she said the thought that gave her strength and comfort was, that she was separated from them for only a short time; she would meet them again and never part. She was able to get up and go about her work again, this glorious truth singing in her heart. Oh, thank God! we are only parted for a time. Cheer up, mourning one. There will be no more sea there.

There are whips and tops and pieces of string,
And little shoes no feet ever wear;
There are bits of ribbon and broken wings,
And tresses of golden hair;

There are dainty jackets that are never worn,
There are toys and models of ships;
There are books and pictures, all faded and torn
And marked by finger tips
Of dimpled hands that have fallen to dust
Yet we strive to think that the Lord is just.

But, as we think of our dear ones dead,
Our children, who never grow old,
And how they are waiting and watching for us
In the city with streets of gold.
And how they are safe through all the years
Form sickness and want and scar,
We thank the great God with falling tears
For the things in the cabinet drawer.

CLEANSING

The sea also speaks of cleansing. What a matchless cleanser the sea is. Think of all the filth and the dirt that flows into it every day all over the world. And still it is so pure. What a hotbed of disease it would become if it failed to absorb this. The reason there will be no more sea there is because there is no filth there. All are pure and spotless, and have no need of cleansing any more

HOW TO START FOR HEAVEN

Are we all on the way? I fear there are those who hope to be there, but they have not started. When are you going to make the start? You want to see the loved ones who have gone before. There is only one way there, and that is the narrow way. Jesus is the way, and no man can come to the Father but by HIM. If you reject Him you shut the door of glory in your own face and open the door to hell. It is a prepared place, and you must be prepared for it by being washed in the Blood of the Lamb. Nothing that defileth entereth there. All are pure and perfect. The conditions of going there are:

Take your place as a guilty, lost, helpless, hopeless, condemned-already sinner, without one plea. Cast yourself unreservedly upon Christ and Christ alone for salvation. Confess with your mouth Jesus as Lord and you will never perish but have everlasting life.

You must be the heir if yonder is your inheritance. You must be the labourer, if yonder is our rest. You must be the candidate, if yonder is your reward. As you now add excellence to excellence, as you are not barren or unfruitful, 'so shall an entrance be ministered to you abundantly into the everlasting kingdom of our Lord Jesus Christ.'

For thee, O dear, dear country,
Mine eyes their vigils keep;
For very love, beholding
Thy happy name, they weep;
The mention of Thy glory
Is unction to the breast,
And medicine in sickness,
And love, and life and rest.

O sweet and blessed country,
The home of God's elect!
O sweet and blessed country,
That eager hearts expect!
Jesus, in mercy bring us
To that dear land of rest,
Who art with God the Father,
And Spirit ever blest.

Christs Second Coming

❖

"Christ was once offered to bear the sins of many; and unto them
that look for Him shall He appear the SECOND time without
sin unto salvation." Hebrews 9: 28

T he second coming of Christ - The hope of the Church - was
held firmly and ardently for the first 300 years by the Christian Church. It was never called in question, but it was the
source of their inspiration in service and comfort and strength
in their persecutions and martyrdom. At any moment, they
believed, the Lord Himself would descend from heaven, and their
sufferings and trials would end.

THE DECLINE

This hope of the Church began to decline and fade away
about the third century. The decline was brought about in three
ways.

(1) By spiritualising and allegorising the fact of His coming again. Origen, one of the early fathers, was the first to teach this. The Lord's coming again seemed delayed to the early believers, until they began to wonder whether they hadn't made a mistake in taking His coming again literally, so when Origen began spiritualising and allegorising it, it helped them to still believe His words and explain the delay. This view of His coming again is largely held by the major denominations of the Church today.

(2) The unholy union of Church and State. When the Emperor Constantine accepted Christianity (or at least professed to do so), Christianity became the national religion of the Roman Empire. They thought the Millennium had come. This must be what Christ meant when He spoke of His coming again to set up His kingdom, so the hope began to die out of their life and belief. This has continued until this day; many believed they will bring in the Millennium through governments and legislation. They think this is what is meant when Jesus said he would come again and set up His kingdom on earth.

(3) The rise of the Papacy. When the Emperor became the head of the Church, or the Pope, they were opposed to any such teaching as Christ coming on earth to reign as King. The Papacy has ever since been the most malignant and hostile opponent of Christ's coming again. They have trampled in the blood of millions of Christians who held this hope. They have ever done their best to blot this hope out. Read the history of the Waldensian Church. They were hunted over the Alps of Italy for centuries, suffering awful privations and martyrdom, rather than yield their belief in the return of our Lord Jesus. Although the decline set in and has continued until this day, yet the coming of our Lord is the immutable word of God and draweth nigh. Hallelujah!

WHAT IS MEANT

When we speak about our Lord's return, and as the Bible teaches it, we mean -

1. THAT IT WILL BE A PERSONAL RETURN

His coming never means a coming of 'someone' or 'something' else, as many would have us believe today. The descent of the Holy Spirit at Pentecost, and since, is not the Second Coming of Christ, because Jesus said HE (not the Holy Spirit) would come again. The angels said, "This **same Jesus** would come in like manner as ye saw Him go" - not someone else but **"this same Jesus"**. The apostle said, "Jesus HIMSELF would descend from heaven." Notice how guarded and emphatic the words are. Not "Jesus shall descend," but "Jesus HIMSELF". You see if we make the Second Coming of Christ anything but personal, we strike a blow at the doctrine of the Trinity, for the Holy Spirit is the third person of the blessed Trinity. Then we are told that when Jesus comes again, the dead in Christ will be the first (that corruption will put on incorruption), then we which are alive and remain will be changed and caught up (This mortal will put on immortality), and together we shall meet the Lord in the air. When the Holy Ghost came at Pentecost and when he comes in power at revivals, the dead are not raised and we are not caught up; so you see how absurd it is to speak of His coming again as anything but a personal return.

2. THAT IT WILL BE A VISIBLE RETURN

Then we also mean, it will be a visible return. We know when He comes **with** His Church to the **earth** to set up the kingdom, every eye will see Him, but when He comes to the air **for** His born again ones (the Church) I wonder whether the unsaved will see Him or only His born again ones? One thing is clear and certain, we who are His saved ones will see Him and we shall be changed "in a moment, in the twinkling of an eye," and we will be for ever with Him and like Him. No wonder our hearts beat faster at the thought of His return. A magnet will only draw the steel filings to itself. The gems and gold will never feel its drawing. So it will be when He comes, the unsaved will never feel or know He has come again, until they miss us and begin to wonder where we have gone to, or what has happened to us. Then anguish and tribulation will come upon them.

3. THAT IT WILL BE A LITERAL RETURN

We also mean His coming again will be literal. That is, it won't be some great historical or national event. Some say that when Jerusalem was destroyed that was the coming of Christ, or what was meant by His coming again. Just imagine comparing Jesus Christ to such a monster as Emperor Titus. Then how ridiculous it is. Christians were not raised from the dead and living ones were not caught up. His second coming will be as LITERAL as His first coming was. It's queer how the old devil changes his tactics. Before Jesus came the first time, he got the Jews to spiritualise His first coming and literalise His second coming. In these "last of the last days" he has got the Church to literalise His first coming and spiritualise or allegorise His second coming. He is always trying to destroy or nullify this blessed hope of the Church and how well he succeeds is evident on every hand today. Let us not be ignorant of his devices.

4. THAT IT WILL BE A PRE-MILLENNIAL RETURN

We also mean His coming again will be pre-millennial. That is He will come **before** the millennium and come to set up the millennium. The Bible never even suggests that the condition of this world when Jesus comes again, will be one of millennial blessedness, but always and only teaches that the world will be a world of awful wickedness, as it was in the days of Noah. Days of violence, corruption, drunkenness and wickedness, **so** shall it be when Jesus comes again. How hopeless and discouraging Christian work would be if we had to win the world for Christ. We are farther from it today than ever. Five-eighths of the world today is lying in heathen darkness, in spite of the Church and her labours for well nigh 2,000 years. Who ever heard of a converted village, or a converted town, let alone a converted city or country? There are very few converted families let alone cities. The mission of the Church is not the conversion of the world, but the gathering out of the Church - the body, the bride of Christ. Then you say the Church and the Gospel is a failure. Oh no. They are accomplishing the work they were called and chosen to do. The Church was never intended to convert the world but to witness to the world. Supposing I started a linen factory and was doing fine - making good linen and selling all I made. You came along and asked me, "How are you doing?" I said, "Fine, business is good." You said, "Are you making and selling any boots?" "No, this isn't a boot factory, this is a linen factory." Just imagine you saying, "Oh, you are a failure. You are not making and selling boots." How ridiculous for anyone to talk like that. It is no more ridiculous than anyone saying that the Church is a failure because she isn't making a better world or saving it. That is not her business. Her business is to witness to all, and the Lord will call out His own. This is being done today. The Lord commanded His disciples and commands us today, "to watch and pray for ye know not the **day** or **hour** when He shall come." This command would be absurd, if the world is to be converted ere He comes and have 1,000 years of millennial blessedness. We know, according to this theory, that He couldn't come for at least another 1,000 years even from today. Then if all the world is to be converted ere He comes, that would mean another 50 years, and only then, if no one failed to win another to Christ. How ridiculous to command us to "watch" and the event so far in the future. We believe Jesus meant exactly what He said, and said exactly what He meant, when He said He would come again.

I was once invited to conduct a city-wide campaign but was asked not to preach on the second coming of Christ, as it was controversial was neither **important** nor **essential.** Certainly I refused the invitation, because I felt they were seeking to rob me of my liberty in Christ. If they invited me, it was surely because they trusted me, and if they trusted me they ought never to have dictated what I was to preach about. At least that is how I felt about it, but what surprised me was the statement, "It is neither important nor essential." I want to look into this and see whether the "Second Coming" of Christ is important and essential.

IMPORTANT AND ESSENTIAL

1. IT IS IMPORTANT

Let us consider this along three lines:

(1) The doctrine of the second coming occupies the largest place in the Bible of any other doctrine. From Genesis to Malachi, and in almost every book there are clear predictions regarding His coming again. Enoch prophesied His coming. Job, a contemporary of Abraham, said He would see Him. Baalam was a premillennialist. Moses, David, the Prophets - major and minor - all declare His coming again. It is very significant, that while His first coming was predicted in detail, hundreds of years before He came, the emphasis is given to His **second** coming, not His first. There are mentions of His **second** coming without

any mentions of His **first** coming. But there is no mention of His **first** coming without, preceding or immediately following, a mention of His **second** coming. The big thing wasn't His **first** coming, according to the Old Testament writers, but His second coming. In fact when Jesus came, they wouldn't believe it. They believed in the literal coming of Christ in glory to reign, but they couldn't believe in His first coming to suffer and die. Then there are some 400 mentions of Christ's second coming in the New Testament, that is, once in every twenty verses. The largest place is given to it in the New Testament. Do you imagine the Holy Spirit would give it such a large place in the Bible if it was an **unimportant** doctrine? Surely not. It is surely given this large place because of its importance and to teach us to give it its place in our thinking and living and preaching.

(2) It is so important **that the Bible will be a sealed book unless we believe in a literal, personal, premillennial return of our Lord.** Many a time we are made to wonder when we read or hear scholarly men, tell us about the mistakes and contradictions of the Bible. Some of the most obvious passages bewilder them and either make them deny their integrity or misinterpret them altogether. You wonder can they be sincere and honest. In fact their sincerity and honesty is not called in question by many and they are therefore led into doubt and denial of the inerrancy of the Bible. Why are the scholars misled and misleading? They surely don't wilfully mislead. No; they don't come to God's Word in the right way, therefore they are misled. Until we see God's plan, and God's Man, in the Bible we will never be able to understand it properly. Have you ever tired to look through a telescope? If you put the wrong end of it to your eye you wonder what sort of a world you are living in. But when you put the right end to your eye and focus it properly, then 50 miles away looks only a mile away. So it is in reading the Bible; if we don't or won't put the right end of the telescope to our eye,

we will never understand it, but will misunderstand and misrepresent it. The personal, literal, pre-millennial return of our Lord is putting the right end of the telescope to our eye when gazing on God's plan for the ages. When we find the **Man** in the Book we will find there are no errors nor contradictions.

A father wondered how he could best entertain his children and yet allow himself freedom to read his paper. He bought a box of blocks with the map of Great Britain on them. He thought this will keep them busy and quiet and let me read my paper. He had hardly settled down to read until they shouted, "We have done it." he was surprised and looked around, and sure enough the map was complete. He said, "You surely have learned your geography well." the youngest child said, "You see, father, there is a picture of a man on the other side, so when we got the man right, the map was right." So it is when reading the Bible, when we get the **Man** in His rightful place in the Bible, then the Bible becomes a divine unity without mistake or error. If this is so, and it is, then how can anyone say the second coming of Christ is unimportant.

(3) It is so important, that **every doctrine of the Bible is associated with it**. This is the Bible incentive for holy living and faithful service. Jesus may return at any moment. How can we live worldly, selfish lives, if we believe it? How can we fail to be active and enthusiastic in His service, if we believe in His near and sure return? Could you give me any better incentive for being faithful in preaching or testifying? Surely we would never wilt before our adversaries or compromise His message, if we believed he was "at hand"? In the midst of persecution and suffering what better incentive could you give men than, "In a moment, in the twinkling of an eye" the Lord will come and reward me? When sorrow's cold and desolating blast hits me and my frail barque is well nigh wrecked, what comfort can you give me like this. "The Lord Himself will descend from heaven," my sorrow will forever cease and I'll meet my loved ones and

meet to part no more? "Wherefore comfort one another with these words," and surely they are suitable ones to do so with. After all this how can anyone say the "Second Coming" of Christ is an unimportant doctrine. Thank God for such a glorious, comforting, purifying hope.

2. IT IS ESSENTIAL

Let us consider another statement. **It is an Essential Doctrine.** I believe man can be saved and not hold scriptural views regarding the second coming of Christ. We are not saved by believing Christ is coming again. We are saved by believing He died "for us men and our sins." So when we speak of it, as being essential we don't mean, essential to salvation, although a saved life without this incentive must be lacking. His coming again is essential -

(1) To Demonstrate His claims to Deity. They would have nothing to do with His claim to Deity when here on earth. They called Him a drunkard, a wine-bibber, a friend of sinners. They scoffed at all His claims and would have none of Him to be their God and Saviour. You remember how anxiously He asked His disciples the question, "Whom say YE that I am?" When they answered He was the Son of God, He rejoiced because they believed His claims. The religious leaders and masses refused His claims. It is the same today; our leaders are willing to acknowledge Him as the greatest teacher, leader, founder, the world has ever known, but so many deny His Deity. Thank God for the few here and there who acknowledge Him as their God and Saviour. If the world is ever to acknowledge His Deity, He must come again and thus demonstrate it. We often sing.

"O *that with yonder sacred throng,*
We at His feet may fall,
Join in the everlasting throng,
And crown Him Lord of all."

There will be no doubt about our being there. Every devil, Satan, all the damned. Angel, archangel, cherubim and seraphim, redeemed hosts, will be there, and EVERY knee shall bow and **every** tongue confess that Jesus is **Lord**. Every minister and theological professor who denied it here will be compelled to confess it that day, to their eternal sorrow and torment, they will confess His Deity. It will be demonstrated that day beyond the shadow of a doubt. If we are to be saved here, we must confess with our MOUTH Jesus as **Lord**. But whether we do so or not, that day of His coming will demonstrate to angels and ages, men and devils that Jesus is **Lord**. So you see how essential His Second coming is.

Then again it is essential,

(2) To make good His claim as King of the Jews. The Jews wouldn't have Him and derided His claim while here on earth. They mocked Him, they put a crown of thorns on His head, a sceptre in His hand, a robe on Him and bowed their knee and spat in His face. When Pilate put the inscription on His cross, "The King of the Jews," they were mad and tried to get Pilate to change it. They said, "**He said** He was King of the Jews." The dying thief recognised Him as King and said, "Remember me when thou comest into thy **kingdom.**" While the mob were mocking and deriding, Pilate said, "Behold your King," but they cried, "Away with Him, away with Him, crucify Him." Mention Jesus to a Jew today and see the look of disgust on his face. If ever the Jews are to believe His is their King, He must come back again - it is essential. Every eye shall see Him and they who pierced Him, then they will know Him as their King and a nation will be born in a day.

It is also essential for Jesus to come again,

(3) To give this old world peace. Since ever sin entered there has been no peace, either in creation or in humanity. It has been strife and hatred, enmity and bitterness. The whole creation groaneth, for the creation was made subject to vanity, not willingly, but by reason of Him who hath subjected the same **in hope**, because creation itself shall also be delivered from the bondage of corruption into the glorious liberty of the children of God. Then there will be universal peace in creation. The lion and the lamb will lie down together. A child shall lead them. Then nations will **learn** war no more, their weapons will be beaten into ploughshares. This world of humanity has never had peace and never will until Jesus comes again - the Prince of Peace. Rulers and governments have tried in all ages to bring about peace amongst all men, but the normal condition has always been and will always be, "wars and rumours of wars." Leagues of nations or NOTIONS, peace treaties have all ended in heart-ache and failure and always will do so, until He comes whose right it is to reign. When He comes then the golden age will dawn and the old world will have 1,000 years of millennial bless-edness and universal peace. If the promises of God are ever to be fulfilled then it is essential Jesus should come again and see them fulfilled.

Again, it is essential Jesus should come again

(4) To complete our salvation. We who are saved are only HALF SAVED. The saved ones in the Glory are only HALF SAVED. They are disembodied spirits. Their bodies are still asleep in the grave. They wait for His coming again in heaven. We wait here on earth, to complete our salvation for our bodies are redeemed as well as our souls, "We ourselves groan within ourselves waiting for the adoption, to wit, the redemption of our body." So If He doesn't come again the saints in heaven and on earth will never be **fully** saved. But, glory to God! When He comes, them also which sleep in Jesus will God bring with Him. Then corruption in the grave will put on incorruption. We which are alive and remain (this mortal) shall put on immortality and together we shall rise to meet our Lord in the air. Hallelujah! Oh, friends, never let us be guilty in word or thought of speaking or thinking that the second coming of Christ is not an essential doctrine. May it increasingly become such to each of us, day by day, as we near His return.

SAVED ONES

What should all this mean to us who love His return and look for it? We should surely see to it that our hearts are pure and clean. "The pure in heart shall see God." If we really believed in His return we wouldn't allow impurity of heart. We should be ashamed before Him at His coming, if we did. Let us therefore cleanse ourselves from all filthiness of the flesh and the spirit, perfecting holiness in the fear of the Lord, for His coming is at hand. We should also live separated lives - "in the world but not of it". What shame would be ours if He came and found us in the show or dance or card party. What shame and loss will be ours if we do not live separated lives. Come out from among them and touch not the unclean thing, is His command to us today as we walk and live as pilgrims and sojourners, as we see the day approaching. Then as we see the signs of His return multiplying on every hand, surely it will make us zealous in His service and doing all we can by all means to save some out of the wreck. We cannot surely be idle or indifferent when we feel His return is so near. We'll seek to have ripened sheaves and not faded leaves when He comes.

UNSAVED ONES

What will happen to every unsaved one when He comes? There will be a separation. Two in bed, one taken, one left. Two grinding corn - one taken, one left. Two in the field - one taken, one left. Tell me, reader, will you be TAKEN or LEFT! His coming is near. The Bible never speaks of it as a YEAR or MONTH or WEEK but in such a DAY such an HOUR. In a MOMENT, in the twinkling of an eye. As sudden as that. He is coming QUICKLY, not SLOWLY. Oh, be ready. The only way to be ready is to repent of your sins now, and receive Him as your personal Saviour, and confess Him openly before others, then when He comes He will confess you before His Father and the angels.

So I'm watching and I'm waiting each moment of the day,
For it may be noon, or evening, when He calleth me away,
And it makes the day go faster, and its trials easier borne,
When I'm saying every moment, **Today the Lord may come.**